MY FATHER'S WAR

A MEMOIR

MY
FATHER'S
WAR

A MEMOIR

JULIA COLLINS

FOUR WALLS EIGHT WINDOWS   NEW YORK / LONDON

PUBLISHED IN THE UNITED STATES BY
Four Walls Eight Windows
39 West 14th Street
New York, NY 10011
http://www.4w8w.com

UK OFFICES:
Four Walls Eight Windows/Turnaround
Unit 3 Olympia Trading Estate
Coburg Road, Wood Green
London N22 6TZ

FIRST PRINTING APRIL 2002

LIBRARY OF CONGRESS CATALOGING-IN-PUBLICATION DATA:
Collins, Julia,
      My father's war : a memoir / Julia Collins.
            p. cm.
      ISBN: 1-56858-224-2
      1. Collins, Jeremiah Frederick. 2. World War, 1939-1945—Veterans—United
States—Biography. 3. Word War, 1939-1945—Campaigns—Japan—Okinawa
Island. 4. United States. Marine Corps—Biography. 5. Collins, Julia. I. Title.

VE25.C65 C653 2002
940.54'28'092—dc21
[B]   2001058558

PRINTED IN THE UNITED STATES

10   9   8   7   6   5   4   3   2   1

FRONTISPIECE: *Jerry Collins in his US Marine Corp uniform*

CONTENTS

MY
FATHER'S
WAR

A MEMOIR

SUITCASE FULL OF MEMORIES

Jerry Collins with some of his intelligence unit comrades at Guadalcanal

Dear Folks:

As I think of it the more I realize what irony was wrought by this war. As to what we accomplished we managed to lose countless good men. It seems the best were taken and the poorer saved. I wonder if men like John Terrence were taken to spare them from this world. I don't think too much of it. Another result has been the great suppression of initiative and ambition of the enlisted men who have had to endure so long now a life when there seems to be no future. I'll be glad to be a civilian again [so] I can take up where I left off in building my future. I'm going to be very interested in how a lot of these people do when they lose the authority temporarily granted by an Act of Congress. At least I know my education equals or excels that of at least 90 percent of the men out here. I'm not worried about my future.... You can rest easy as far as taking care of myself goes. I'm pretty good at it.

Love to you all,
Jerry

(From a letter posted from Guam, August 25, 1945, eleven days after Japan surrendered, two and a half weeks after the United States dropped the first atom bomb, and two months after his intelligence unit fought on Okinawa, the bloodiest island battle of World War II, the greatest land-sea-air battle in history.)

"Thank god! Now listen up," he said in a hoarse whisper the moment he spotted me. "We've got to get out of here. I took a hit. I'm hurt bad, so it's up to you."

I stood there dumbstruck while my father, oblivious to blinking hospital monitors and IV lines, told me how we would manage his escape from this prison camp and what my job would be. He called me "buddy" and it was clear that he put all his faith in me, to get him out of this hellhole.

"What are you waiting for?" He made a move to reach out and grab me, or maybe to whack me into action, but his twig of an arm fell back against his side and stuck there useless. That's when I finally shook off the shock of his appearance: the burning eyes in a skeletal head, his every muscle taut. His six-foot-two frame was so wasted it barely lifted the covers. I tried to calm him down, touching his hot hand with my cool one, brushing the hair off his forehead, but that only infuriated him. He went rigid with frustration, his expression changing from trusting to wary.

"Shut your trap. They'll hear us," he hissed, twisting his neck to see beyond me. "Jesus almighty." The pain of his chest wound knotted his face. "I can't move at all. You've got to stash me some-place quick. Then you go get help. They'll be back any minute."

"No, they won't. You're safe here. I promise."

He looked at me intently. "Don't let them fool you," he said urgently, explaining how the doctors were Japanese soldiers in dis-guise. "Japs," he called them. "They infiltrated last night. They've got this room hidden away"—he couldn't speak for a moment. "You won't believe what goes on in there. They strapped me down and tore me open. When they come back they're going to finish me. They'll cut me to ribbons. Pull out my guts. Bash my skull open and rearrange my brains. I know what I'm talking about." He clenched his jaw to hold back tears, terrified.

"Oh, Dad," I said mournfully. I clenched my jaw too and bent over him. He stared back at me, his eyes too dark and deep for me to see what really lurked inside. The silver stubble on his face shimmered in the pallid light. His skin was waxy and yellow. The lines running from that big old nose of his down along either side of his sunken mouth had turned into slashes. He looked like a goner. Close up like this, I could see the lurid surgi-cal slice, the staples holding his chest together. The aortic aneurysm hadn't killed him, but the hole they discovered in his heart was a dire complication. It had been there all his life, his body's dreadful secret.

"Dad, it's Julie. Your daughter. Nobody's going to hurt you. I'm right here and Mom will be back any minute. Those are real doctors. One of them saved your life." I told him he was in a bed, safe and sound, at Yale New Haven Hospital. The surgery was over, an unexpected success, and before long he would be home again, in good old Branford.

He glared at me while I babbled on, betraying him with my cowardly refusal to grab his gurney and run for cover. I sure as hell was no Marine, I was worse than an Army doggie, much worse.

"Get me a knife, then," he said. "I'll look out for myself. Get me a knife right now, you shit head."

I glared back at him, ridiculously offended by this broken-down Marine. There was no reaching the stubborn bastard.

"Please!" He was begging for his life.

The nice-looking nurse on duty bustled in, smiling at both of us, greeting my deranged parent as if he were her delightful pal. He bayoneted her with his eyes and I saw how he shrank against the bed. She asked me to leave for a few minutes, so she could tend to him.

"Dad, it's okay," I said, backing out of the room. "It really is okay. I'll be right here."

"Go to hell. I can take care of myself."

With high-tech medical weaponry all around me I stood crying in the hub of the intensive care unit, where my father was one among many hard cases, but the only one, I'm certain, who believed he'd gotten his wounds in combat with the Japanese.

Through the glass I saw him lying there like a poor dumb lab animal, completely clueless about what the hell was happening. I had only arrived an hour ago and already I had failed him. As a daughter with only comfort to offer I was useless; what he demanded was rescue. Marines never left their wounded behind.

Before long the nurse came out, no longer cheery. She said Dad's doctors would adjust his medication, which should stop the hallucinations that had landed him back on the bloody island of his World War II nightmares. A lot of people get confused and upset on the drugs my father was taking, she told me in a soothing professional manner.

You'd better be right, I thought.

I became furious with my father. What a pain-in-the-ass patient he was! He hadn't gone to a doctor in fifty years, pigheadedly refusing to take care of himself. Now look at him. After surviving the stitching of his backed-up heart and the roto-rootering of his gunked-up lungs, he'd gone looney-toons on us. And I had to be back in Boston on Monday. If he didn't snap out of it soon, things were going to spin out of control again. This family could not cope with another disaster.

That was early December. In February I sat in Dad's bedroom, upstairs in the old grey house in the town where we both were born and grew up. It was the middle of the night. My heartbroken mother was asleep downstairs; we were the only two in the house. Other family members would start arriving the next day to prepare for the funeral and dispose of my father's belongings. That wouldn't take long: he owned almost nothing.

The upstairs was unheated, and I shivered in my father's ratty T-shirt. I'd rushed home that afternoon without bringing a toothbrush or clothing, bombing down 90 and 295 and 95 and finally Pine Orchard Road as I imagined over and over my Dad's last minutes on earth, before he turned his face to the hospital wall and said: Enough. No more surgery. He was shipping out.

He died around noontime, right after my mother left. She had given her ex-husband a kiss and said in her chipper way, "I'll be back after work, Jerry darling!" She had barely reached her office a couple of miles away when she was summoned back to the hospital.

And that's when I called, just missing her, and made her coworker tell me what I already knew.

The dusty carpet in Dad's room reeked of ten thousand Kools. I reached under the bed, snagged the handle and pulled. A battered brown suitcase emerged. It was the last of my mother's maiden luggage set, with BG monogrammed in gilt on the cracking leather. At one time a snazzy little traveling companion, now a worn-out piece of junk with no place to go, a sadly suitable repository for my father's few treasures.

The only working light was a metal desk lamp, so I stuck it on the bed and aimed its hot beam at the suitcase on the floor. I had never looked inside before. Over the years I'd occasionally found Dad poring over its contents, sitting on this bed. I always tried to sneak away before he caught me watching him from the doorway. I knew at those times he was trying to leave us all behind, forget we ever existed, lose himself as we knew him. That suitcase was Dad's passage out of the present and back to the days when he was still an optimistic young man with big dreams, the only son of a loving family, an aspiring student at Yale, a brave Marine who put his life on the line alongside his buddies.

The brass latch snapped open. I lifted the lid and stared at the heaps of letters, black-and-white photos, a glossy color portrait of FDR, and documents. One declared the honorable discharge from the United States Marine Corps Reserve of Corporal Jeremiah Frederick Collins on April 18, 1946—eleven months after the collapse of the Third Reich and nine months after the radio broadcast of Japanese Emperor Hirohito's surrender.

I touched the envelopes brown with age, all addressed in a youthful version of my father's spiky cursive. It was startling to see what a prolific correspondent young Jerry Collins had been. From boot camp on Parris Island to combat in the Southeast Pacific to his tour of occupation in China, Private First Class then Corporal

Collins had lovingly written every few days to his mother, father, and younger sister back home in Branford. There were more than two and a half years' worth of letters. I would later count 237 of them. My grandmother had saved every last missive, and after her death in the 1970s he reclaimed them.

Dad's Marine knife was also in the suitcase, but his ribbons and medals were gone. I had counted on seeing them. Where could they be? Then I remembered: he'd thrown them out years earlier, in a fit of melancholy, along with his fatigue cap and his uniforms. Nobody was around to stop him. He probably would have thrown away everything in the suitcase too, if it hadn't been in his mother's safekeeping at the time.

The loose windowpanes shook as the wind battered against the house, which seemed very frail that night. My stiffening fingers made it hard to open the envelopes. In the morning I would be found by my mother, cold and alone with Dad's letters scattered about me like frostbitten leaves. I pulled one out and started to read but I couldn't continue past "Dear Folksies."

His presence was overwhelming. The body cooling over at Clancy's Funeral Home, awaiting cremation—that wasn't Dad. That body belonged to a broken-down elderly man. My father was the whip-thin young Marine in the fifty-year-old photographs, aiming his Browning Automatic Rifle at boot camp, wearing his dress uniform to impress the folks back home, standing with a couple of buddies in front of the mess tent on Guadalcanal.

Suddenly I remembered another photo. Dad had shown it to me years ago, and I had seen him staring into it many times. It better be here, I worried, and was thrilled to find it: the snapshot of Jerry Collins and comrades in the elite Intelligence Section, Second Battalion, Twenty-ninth Marine Regiment, Sixth Division USMC. They're all stripped to the waist with dog tags dangling, and their bodies are hardened and tan. My father crouches at the center, one of the tallest of the bunch, a typically lean fighting Marine. He's the only one wearing his cap, rakishly set on his handsome head. He looks a good decade older than did that fawn-eyed boy who left Branford in 1943, only two years earlier. A white flash has obliterated part of the picture, just above Dad's head, turning some of the men into ghosts.

Holding it for the first time, I noticed the photo's edges were velvety, the image worn away in places, from being clutched so often between Dad's fingertips. I studied the fading faces, trying to remember who was who. This was my father's wartime family, the buddies he trained with on Guadalcanal and fought next to on Okinawa and Sugar Loaf Hill, during the Pacific theater's bloodiest combat, where more than 80 percent of his regiment died. When all was said and done, 14 percent of all Marines killed in World War II died on Okinawa.

Months after the war ended my lucky father finally returned home, met my mother and got married, and fathered five children. But something irrevocable had happened to the boy famous for his energy and ambition, and for whom high school classmates had predicted a career as a world-renowned chemist. His life came to a standstill, the clock stopping in 1946. He had brought the war home, where it grew inside him, usurping part of his soul. With that self-abnegation typical of World War II vets, Dad didn't let on to his wife, parents, or three sons about the nightmares and survivor's guilt that haunted him. He began to lose himself in booze and other diversions. Eventually, however, as he hit middle age and saw that all his plans were coming to naught, Jeremiah Collins was driven to share his war, in full bloody splendor, with his two youngest children, both daughters.

And I, the wary elder daughter who found it hard to love her father, embarrassed by his failures, disgusted by his follies, came to understand, accept, and finally to respect him through his war. It was the central motif and mystery of our troubled bond.

Over time, I realized my father was not alone in his defeat. There were many other vets like him, emotionally and invisibly scarred by the "Good War," who failed to live up to the impossible standards set for men of their era. I was lucky, in fact, to be Dad's confidant. Most loved ones were kept in the dark. World War II vets are notoriously closemouthed, the stoic product of the Great Depression and wartime when ideals of honor, courage, patriotism, sacrifice, and self-reliance fostered impregnable reticence. The "leatherneck" Marines had an extra burden, given their steely reputation as an elite fighting force. Only now, in old age, have many of these men begun to talk openly about just how bad the Good War was for them.

But on the night Dad died I didn't feel lucky. I abruptly packed up the suitcase and shoved it back under the bed. I'd had enough of my father's war. All my life he'd fed it to me bit by bit, like spoonfuls of Spam, till I got used to the taste. It would be years before I could bring myself to open that suitcase again and add its memories to my own.

CHAPTER ONE THE
LULLABY HOUR

Jerry Collins with his daughter Julia

Which of us has looked into his father's heart?

(Thomas Wolfe, *Look Homeward, Angel*)

Summer twilight found two small sisters with matching pixie hair-cuts tucked into matching iron cots upstairs in the nursery at 101 Pine Orchard Road. I was four going on five and Jennifer was two, and we lay there wide-eyed and buzzing, all tangled up in our flow-ered nightgowns, mine blooming in pink, hers in blue, swaddled in our soft, ancient sheets, and spooked by the shadows waving to us from the walls as the minutes sashayed by, taking their sweet time.

Our house was full of alarming rappings, rustlings, shufflings, creepings, knuckle-crackings, and other unearthly sounds. The attic above our heads was a cobwebby cavern under the rafters where the dark forces gathered. We two prisoners, forgotten by all, clung through thin walls and floorboards to the reassuring murmurs of our mother and father downstairs, Perry Mason speaking loudly to our grandmother, and the commotion of our three big brothers Jeremiah, Patrick, and Peter coming and going as they pleased. They were "the boys," privileged by age and gender; we were "the girls," consigned to squirt-dom, and our family of seven lived with my father's mother, whom we all called Angy, in a saggy farmhouse that I adored, blissfully blind to the leaking roof and buckling plaster that caused my mom such shame and woe.

This was the midsixties, not yet much different from the fifties. Divorce was still a black mark on one's character, especially a woman's, and the family pecking order landed children squarely on the lowest tier, with the youngest at the very bottom. And so, though both our parents were pushovers, not in the least strict, my sister and I went up to bed when we were told to, obediently lan-guishing on marshmallowy old mattresses while the July sun blazed on, and the birch and maple glowed green just outside the window.

It was our mother who heard us say our nightly prayers, the Lord's Prayer, Hail Mary, and this one: "Now I lay me down to sleep I pray the lord my soul to keep if I should die before I wake I pray the lord my soul to take God bless Mommy and Daddy and Chippy and Ricky and Peter and Bobki and Dzazhiu and Angy and Pop and Aunty Alice and Uncle Bill and all our other friends and relatives and all the angels and saints and keep me a good little girl forever and ever amen!"

Then she kissed us goodnight, sealing us in till morning. But after some time had passed, our father usually made his way up the steep squawking stairs, through the master bedroom and on into our musty nook. He stood still in the doorway for a long moment, studying the two small mummies for signs of life. If Jennifer, whom I called "Miff," had fallen asleep already, he kissed his fingers and whispered "nighty-night," leaving me at the mercy of the endless dusk. But if both daughters were awake he came all the way into the room.

He towered in the low-ceilinged nursery, his endless legs like two exclamation points. Back then Dad was a dashing fellow with impeccable posture and a way of standing apart from others, as if he had one foot in some other place. A hint of arrogance and disdain hovered about him in public like eau de cologne. He was elegant in a suit, but Bermuda shorts revealed his legs were two sticks, grotesque with scarring and pitting and reddening of the flesh from jungle rot and a couple of shrapnel wounds he got in World War II.

Forty-two years old, my father had brown hair so dark it looked black. He wore it slicked back off his high forehead, exactly as he had in high school, exactly as he would for the rest of his life. Two of his children inherited his chocolate brown eyes and he passed his mighty prow of a nose on to his youngest son. His slender face with its steep thoughtful forehead appeared somber most

of the time, but sometimes, in his goofy moods, he became the spitting image of Alfalfa, that scrawny, saucer-eyed crooner with the
militant cowlick, one of the Little Rascals in the "Our Gang"
comedies of the twenties and thirties.

"You girls still carousing?!" Dad feigned shock and dismay as
he sat alongside my sister, who I could tell even then was his favorite
child, the youngest and merriest, with big bright eyes and hair
matching his. He ruffled his Miffer-mouse's mop and reached out a
long arm to ruffle mine, which was honey colored but darkening
quickly, like my moods. Then he talked to us for a while, softly, as if
everything were a secret shared by us three only. In that peaceful
room, with his doting, easy-to-please daughters, he set aside the
loud cockiness and defensive airs he projected by day. He became
pensive, his thoughts clearly wandering in and out of the nursery.

When he seemed ready to jump ship, one of us would cajole,
"Daddy, sing 'Cowboy Joe'!" He always complied, slinging his fine
baritone into a jazzy rendition of our favorite bedtime song. He
was a cross between Tony Bennett and Bobby Darin, beating out the
rhythm of a horse's gait on his skinny shanks:

See how he swings
Back and forth in the saddle as he sings,
Raggy music to his cattle on a horse,
A pretty good horse!
With a syncopated gait.
Such a funny meter
To the roar of his repeater.
How they run,
When they hear this feller's gun,
Because the western folk all know:
He's a rootin-tootin, highfalutin
Son-of-a-gun from Arizona,

Ragtime cowboy,
Talk about your cowboy,
Ragtime Cowboy Joe!

His mood lightened as he sang. He grew almost giddy as we cheered him on—"Another! Another!" and he swung into "Here's the story 'bout Minnie the Moocher! She was a low-down hootchie-cootcher!" Or "Pardon me boys! Is that the Chattanooga Choo-Choo?" Or "She's got two left feet but oh-so-sweet is Sweet Georgia Brown!" Or "If Beale Street could talk! There'd be a lot of married men who'd have to take their bed and walk!" Or "On the sidewalk Sunday morning lies a body oozin' life! Someone's sneakin' round the corner! Could that someone be Mack the Knife?" Or "Once I built a railroad. Made it run. Made it race against time. Fifty million boots went slogging through hell! Brother, can you spare a dime?"

As the windowpanes went from gold to grey, he grew bored and weary of fatherhood and thought it was high time his two little "pests" conked out. So he cagily switched to his slow songs: "When It's Sleepy Time Down South," "A Kiss to Build a Dream On," "Bye, Bye, Blackbird," or, heaven forbid, "The Little Dustman," an insipid lullaby I loathed, about a creepy character that spied on children and sprinkled them with sleeping dust.

If that didn't work, and it rarely did, he resorted to telling stories without bothering with the books, carelessly reconstructing vignettes from *Winnie the Pooh* or assorted fairy tales. He kept them short and speedy, barely coherent in details. He raced through Pooh's mishap with the honey pot, leaving Christopher Robin out entirely, he chopped Little Red Riding Hood's dialogue with the Big Bad Wolf, and he mangled the sequence of wishes in *The Fisherman's Wife*.

By this time my toddler sister had dropped off or lay with eyelids at half mast, stupefied by our father's dreadful, sloppy story-telling, while I, two and a half years older, managed to hang onto wakefulness. "And dat's de end of dat! Sweet dreams, kiddos," he finally announced. Two pecks on the forehead and he was gone, the door sighing shut behind him.

But sometimes he lingered till I was sliding in and out of consciousness. As night arrived and turned him into a shadow, he began to tell a strange and mesmerizing story that seemed to run on with no ending, about an island populated by armies of land crabs and poisonous snakes, a homesick Yankee Marine swimming in December in a warm ocean under the Southern Cross, living with buddies in tents like boy scouts, running through the jungle with his rifle, lying sleepless in a wet hole on a blackened hill, praying hopelessly for dawn as the enemy catcalled taunts across the line, shells whistled overhead, and the sky exploded into screaming fire.... I was pulled back from sleep to listen, rapt and uneasy, as his low murmuring voice spun out scenes that grew progressively darker and scarier. My father wasn't paying any attention to his little girls now. He'd forgotten we existed.

Then all at once he was clutching his head in his hands and breathing hard through his nose, his back slumped over. I gaped at him, too petrified to make a peep.

Eventually he got up stiffly and left without a glance or a word. Alone again, my nearby sister a peaceful cocoon, I worked to distract myself, but my father's anguish lingered in the room like a bitter scent. I concentrated fiercely on the world beyond, the farther off the better. I seized upon the mundane noises of our neighborhood slowing down for the night. The few birds still awake twittered weakly. The occasional barking dog gave up quickly. The last of the raucous older kids hanging out on Collins Drive were summoned into their houses. Then one shrill father, an infamous loudmouth, abruptly disturbed the peace with a yelping tirade. As soon as he shut up, the chorus of crickets raised their volume, the peepers chiming in sweetly.

A white moon was out, gauzy and uncertain. Just below the nursery window, I heard footsteps in the driveway and the hiss of a match. "Daddy," I mumbled, struggling to get out of bed and go down to him. My little body, impossibly leaden, sank deeper into the bottomless mattress as sleep overtook me. The distant call of the night train at first kept me company: I'm coming for you! I'm coming for you! But then the whistle turned into a shrill and hostile whining.

My skin prickled with dread. I opened my eyes slowly. The nursery had vanished, my sleeping sister with it, and my own bed too. I was alone, a pip-squeak cowering in a vast emptiness. The whining grew louder. I looked up and saw a silver pineapple come spinning through the black void. It flew right at me, sizzling noisily and throwing off sparks. I was mesmerized, unable to move. At the last second it missed me, whizzing over my head like a bad pitch. But another was coming, and another—the sky was full of silver pineapples. I began flapping my arms madly to bat them away. One struck me head on, exploding, and I fell backward, an intense white light illuminating bodies lying all around me. I hit the ground and woke up mewing and soaked in tears and sweat.

There were many nights like this, when the cozy innocence of the lullaby hour turned into a siege of sadness and nightmares. Each time my father came to bid goodnight, I never knew whether he would depart quickly, still merry, or stay till he became the brooding storyteller who unwittingly fueled my bad dreams. The menacing fruit sequence, as odd as it sounds, was my first nightmare inspired by my father's war, and it repeated over and over again. Dad had told me how the metal casing of a hand grenade looked like the skin of a pineapple. He carried hand grenades when he was a Marine, dangling from his belt, and had to be ready in a flash to flip one toward the enemy—who might attack at any time! He had mimed for me how he armed and threw the grenade, counting slowly and carefully.

At the time I didn't comprehend enemy; in my dream those vicious pineapples *were* the enemy and I was their target.

At four going on five, saucer-eyed and shaking in my bed, I already understood that I must keep these nightmares to myself. I couldn't cry over the pineapple dream with my mother, or I'd betray my father. I couldn't talk to him about it either, or he would feel bad and drop his head into his hands again. I had intuited that my mother couldn't help, and that asking my father would only drive him further into his own dark realm.

On those interminable summer nights, when my dreams did their worst, I fought my way back to sleep. And each morning, arising bleary and apprehensive, I was overjoyed to find my world was radiant and normal again, my dad just like other dads, my family complete. At breakfast my parents behaved nicely toward each other, and the rest of the family seemed oblivious to anything amiss. Hugely relieved, I drank my Cocoa-Marsh and ate my French toast. Wandering outside I saw that my grandmother's orange daylilies and her banks of roses in every shade of lipstick had all decided to bloom together. The Bartlett pear tree showed off its attractive, inedible fruit and the hump-backed plum tree drooped with exotic blossoms. The birds were going wild with joy, racing from branch to branch. My mother eyed a few of them apprehensively as she hung out the glistening-wet bedsheets. My chattering sister squatted like a plump mushroom by the clothes basket, busying herself plucking clothespins one by one from the bucket and dropping them onto the ground. I came swishing toward her through thick, deliciously cool grass above my ankles. Soon my father would be out pushing his lawnmower and whistling cheerfully, just like all the other men in our neighborhood.

CHAPTER TWO

BOOT CAMP

Young Jerry Collins with his pet goat

Yale University has been informed by Marine Corps Headquarters that you will be called to active duty for officer training at Parris Island on or about July first rather than being returned to Yale under navy college training program you should receive your orders within ten days

(Western Union telegram to Jeremiah Frederick Collins, June 14, 1943)

On the morning I started first grade, my daddy, who was a clever cartoonist, with a crudely feisty Li'l Abner sort of style, presented me with a drawing. It was a picture of me dressed in my first-day-of-school outfit: combat helmet, baggy fatigues, and clunky military-style boots, which he told me were 'dockers, short for boondockers, the footwear of World War II Marines. In one hand I carried a lunchbox, in the other a grenade, and I had a gun, an M-I he said, slung over my shoulder. In a spirit of celebration my father had drawn a perky daisy springing from atop my helmet and decorated my M-I with a big bow.

I waited for the bus that September day with trepidation. Our town was undergoing an intense growth spurt and the school system was flooded with children. The smell of fresh tar congealing on newly cut streets and the din of sawing and hammering coming from the ranch, splanch, and ersatz modernist houses rising up all around seemed perpetual. Through some unlucky redistricting maneuver, after kindergarten I was pulled from the rest of the neighborhood kids attending Pine Orchard School and shipped off to a different one farther away. From first grade until high school, like a military brat I rarely stayed more than one year at the same school, leaving behind a trail of half-formed friendships. My battling, distracted parents didn't seem to notice that each Labor Day found me tensely preparing to land on foreign soil.

At least I had two things to cheer me on as I nervously set off for day one: my father's annual cartoon of me geared up for battle and my mother's affectionate notes scrawled in Magic Marker on the skin of the banana or orange she packed in my lunchbox. Actually, Dad did depart from his favorite motif from time to time, drawing me as a jack-o-lantern-toothed, dog patch resident in a granny dress and Minnie Pearl hat smoking a corncob pipe, say, or a ragtag hobo wearing a sandwich board and clutching a bottle of hooch.

"So, how was boot camp?" he asked, after one of my first long days as a first grader. I knew very well what boot camp was, and I supposed he meant that my new school was another sort of endurance test. When Dad arrived at boot camp in 1943, one of a busload of lambs to the slaughter, a crowd of brand-new Marines had welcomed them with a jeer: "You'll be sooooooooooooooooo-oooooooooooorry!" Said my father: "I quaked in my boots. Everybody was barking at us, like a bunch of hyenas. But I expected it to be rough. It wasn't too long before I got the hang of it, all the drilling and running around they made us do." Marine boot camp was notorious for its merciless hammering of new recruits, and it pleased Dad to remember how well one spindly, overtall, undermuscled flamingo-legged boy from Branford held up under the hazing.

He had already drilled me on several occasions, showing me how to march like a Marine while counting off in a rhythmic, nearly unintelligible chant. Now that my sister Miff was three, he drilled her a little too. We marched up and down the gravel driveway, making wobbly turns on our heels so we wound up facing the wrong way. I couldn't get the hang of it, which vastly amused my father. "You've got two left feet, Collins!" he barked. He meant to be funny but I was wounded and wished we could stop.

"And if you think marching's tricky," he continued, "try performing rifle maneuvers at the same time while the DI"—that's drill instructor—"is screaming on and on how you're all a bunch of lousy screwups! Now watch me!" We cleared out of Dad's way and he smartly demonstrated at a stiff cadence, using a long-handled feather duster in place of a rifle, which he snapped from shoulder to shoulder, side to side, up and down, swinging and snapping the duster in front of him with crisp perfection.

Then it was our turn. "One false move," he warned, watching us skitter across the gravel, "and you're on your hands and knees cleaning all the toilets with a toothbrush or running around in circles with a full pack, holding your rifle way up over your head till you're ready to drop! Even worse, if you foul up on some maneuver then your whole platoon has to pay, doing it over and over again till EVERYBODY'S got it right. Not the best way to become popular."

I stared at my dad, mystified, when he told his boot camp stories and put us through our paces. What did he want from us? What was he looking for? The nasty life he described, of getting up before dawn, marching and training in the dust under the hot sun all day, studying by night, constantly hungry and flea-bitten, homesick and bored, with no freedom of movement, forced to tolerate abuse both steady and shockingly unpredictable, like when the DI shoved his face into yours and roared like a bull to ream you for God-knows-what minor infraction while you waited and sweated even harder, fearing whatever physical torment or public humiliation he had in mind for punishment—why did Dad talk about it so much? When he did, invariably his expression became tight and distant, his playful side vanished, and his two little girls marching like ninnies were fuzzy, unsatisfactory stand-ins for the vivid memories hauling him back in time.

Going on six years old, I was still an adoring daughter, yearning to please, but I no longer entirely trusted my daddy. I knew he was revealing things he shouldn't, stoking my frequent nightmares. The flaming pineapples had become real grenades that tore into flesh. I now understood the concept of enemy, the yellow-skinned and sinister Japanese soldier my father still feared. Thanks to him I dreamed of the Divine Wind, the kamikaze fighter planes piloted by fanatics who committed suicide for their Emperor by dive-bombing straight into American naval targets. I dreamed of mud and blood and rotting bodies with missing faces and limbs blown off. Some were my father's close buddies or people he had known and liked or people he hadn't known at all or liked one bit but still mourned with a raw sadness that never scabbed over or healed. He cried for these men when he put on his uniform for the Memorial Day parade. He told me some of their names, and how they died, and I blotted them out as soon as I could, begging for a tiny American flag, a fuzzy blue monkey on a stick, a paper cone topped with pink cotton candy.

When my father was a boy he had an affectionate pet goat he adored named Maisie. She tolerantly hauled him around in a cart until he grew too heavy and walked alongside her instead. An antique photograph on my wall shows this chummy pair setting off together in the vast untamed field that once spread like a grassy sea behind the house on Pine Orchard Road. There's a fleeting quality to this idyllic scene, to the carefree smile on my father's face, captured as he and Maisie turned to stare into the camera. Soon the happy boy, his amiable goat, that generous sweep of land would all be gone. Now, in place of the boy, a grim, hollow-faced man in combat helmet and filthy fatigues staggers into the frame, with the distinctive bow-legged, bent-over lope of the heavily burdened Marine. Holding a rifle instead of a herding stick, he's slogging through knee-high mud across the blasted terrain blanketed with spent mortars and fresh corpses frantically rotting in the subtropical heat, the sky still smoking overhead.

The long-lost child of the photo reminds me of a sappy scrap of verse by John Greenleaf Whittier that Dad liked to quote in a hammy, melodramatic Barrymore manner that always hid his true sentiments: "Blessings on thee little man, barefoot boy with cheeks of tan! With thy turned-up pantaloons, and thy merry whistled tunes!" In his mocking way I think my father mourned that child in tinted sepia, a small-town innocent bumped off in the war—"O for boyhood's painless play..."

Jeremiah Frederick Collins, known to all as Jerry, was born in 1922 and grew up in rural Branford, Connecticut, on the mirror-still waters of Long Island Sound. My father was proud of his hometown, which claims a brief page of colonial history. Shortly after the Pequot War the New Haven Colony purchased the land that became Branford in 1638 from the warrior Montowese, ruler of the Mattabesec, an Algonquian tribe, for "eleven coats of trucking cloth and one coat of English cloth, made in the English fashion." Originally called Totoket, an Indian name that means "the Land of the Tidal River," the town was formally settled by some thirty-odd Puritan families in 1644. They prized its harbor, generous pasturage and woodland, and fertile agricultural land. Relations with local Indians were generally amicable and the town prospered. Trading up and down the coast and in the West Indies along with shipbuilding became important local industries. In the 1700s wealthier Branford residents were importing numerous slaves to the town—though few remained by the time Connecticut abolished slavery in 1848. During the revolution eleven Branford men dashed off to Boston to serve as Minutemen. Many others helped defend New Haven from British attack in 1779. The patriotic town even had its own warship, the *New Defense*. After the war, Branford shifted to an industrial economy and a number of local mills and manufacturing concerns sprang up.

By the 1840s the bustling town that had briefly rivaled New Haven began to slow down. Long after its boom time, however, Branford kept its attractive reputation for unpretentious good living. It lacked the Currier and Ives quaintness of Guilford and Madison, its neighbors up the coast, evolving instead into a more democratic blend of blue-collar and genteel, from its towering nineteenth-century mill to its filigreed and turreted Victorian showplaces over-looking the Sound from Indian Neck. Branford looked well lived in rather than antique, its past recorded in its factories and fields, stately churches on the green, fishing boats and summer cottages, cemeteries crowded with centuries of solid citizens, and place names mingling Plant and Hotchkiss with Montowese and Yowago.

The town meandered attractively along a cursive coastline, the picturesque Thimble Islands always in view, numbering from several dozen to one for every day in the year, depending on how one cate-gorized the bare rocks where seabirds congregated. According to folklore, the notorious but incompetent pirate Captain Kidd lurked among these islands shortly before he was captured in Boston and sent off to London for hanging in 1701. Branford's far-flung villages boasted small beaches of fine gold sand, including Branford Point, where Jerry Collins and his family went swimming every summer. Plentiful woods and open land remained for children to explore, yet the fortunate proximity of New Haven, with its university, sym-phony, shops, restaurants, and theater kept the town from becom-ing a backwater. One could hop on the trolley and go all the way into the city even from the remotest edge of town, Stony Creek, where the tracks sliced straight through the whispering salt marsh, not far from the granite quarries in operation since the late 1800s.

In my dad's day, Model Ts rattled along elm-lined Main Street past the shops wearing their fancy false fronts, past Branford Green with its white-columned town hall, Civil War Monument, and collection of Protestant churches, and on to the domed marble splendor of the 1896 James Blackstone Memorial Library, the gift of a railroad magnate. Across the street rose the gold brick, neo-Romanesque tower of St. Mary Church, where the Catholic Collinses did their praying.

Without a doubt Dad had a happy start in life, a sunny Little Rascals youth in a Norman Rockwell setting. The way he told it, his childhood was an endless round of games and hijinks with the neighborhood kids, who all had nicknames like Fatty and Mac and Butchie. Mothers opened backdoors, boys and girls dashed out, and for hours on end they played and cavorted unchecked. Hearing Dad wax nostalgic about his young years you'd think there was no Depression going on, but I learned later, partly through the grown-up voice of his wartime letters, that his parents in fact were always working and scrimping and worrying about money. They just happened to know how to have a good time, too.

The elder Jeremiah Collins co-owned a hardware store on Main Street, called Collins & Freeman, which sold "hardware, radio, and farm supplies" along with paints, glass, and household goods. By all accounts my grandfather, whom I never got to meet, was a kind-hearted and jovial fellow who often talked around a cigar. "Pop" had some unusual qualities for a man of his day: along with sports, cars, and his daily newspapers, he enjoyed gardening, preparing feasts, and brewing beer with his wife, Alice, who was a gourmet cook. He also encouraged her passions for music and theater—even, on occasion, performing opposite her—and her yen to be a woman about town, at the wheel of her own automobile.

Vivacious, strong willed, and cheerily self-centered, Alice had been a modestly successful chanteuse in her youth. As a married woman she sang opera and operetta in local productions and organized some of the WPA musical performances that kept players working. She founded the town's Musical Art Society, still active today, and was the organist for St. Mary Church from my father's boyhood until the 1970s. She was also the undisputed ringer in the church choir, and at home would burst into song unpredictably highbrow or bawdy, as Brownie the cocker spaniel howled along. Dad mimicked for me how his mother's mighty soprano had regularly summoned him from across the neighborhood—"Jee-AIR-eeeeeeee! DiIIIIIner's Red-EEEEEEEE!"—her Valkyrie cry echoing forever as she clanged the bell by the back door and he streaked home on the wings of Mercury to shut her up.

Young Jerry Collins was a bright and whimsical boy who loved practical jokes—he later taught me how to short sheet a bed, position a pail of water on a doorjamb, and other such stunts. He was also a tenderhearted fellow who suffered whenever an animal raised by the family wound up on the dinner table. One evening a glance from the platter to his mother's guilty expression told him another pet had been sacrificed and he yelped, aghast, "That's Bunny-Wunny!" before running from the table. My father never forgot the time a relative insisted he learn how to slaughter a chicken. His eyes clouded up thirty years later when he described how the chicken struggled while he tried to wring its neck, hands shaking, eyes averted, till his impatient relative grabbed the bird and—crack!—finished it off.

Dad adored, protected, and teased his younger sister Alice, who was pretty and sweet, and, like her brother, tougher than she looked. Alice was plump as a dove, however, whereas Jerry was a skinny beanpole with spaghetti limbs. He wistfully fumbled through sports, except basketball, where his height came in handy. In variety shows and recitals, egged on by his limelight-loving mother, he reluctantly exposed natural talents at playing the piano, singing, and hoofing. But although he was no Jack Armstrong All-American Boy on the playing field, Jerry did have one advantage over the jocks: he was one of the first boys in town to cruise around in his own jalopy, a rattletrap that broke down every few miles.

My father spent his early childhood in a modest house on a quiet street at the center of town. Eventually, when the last of the elder Collinses died, Jeremiah Sr. moved his wife and two children to the Collins homestead two miles away. Dad's grandfather, Michael Collins, had built the house in the 1870s. Michael left western Ireland in the wake of the potato famine, settled in Branford with his wife, Ellen Gilhooley Collins, and had four children, my Dad's Uncle Dennis and Aunts Nellie and Hannah, and Dad's father, Jeremiah Joseph, who was born at home during the famous Blizzard of 1888.

Michael Collins wasn't much of a builder, and whoever helped him was equally slapdash. Probably time and money were tight, which explains the dank hole of a cellar, cheap choices of materials, and overall lack of elegant detail. Or maybe the Irish emigrant was in love with the huge swath of land he now possessed, and regarded the farmhouse as a necessity not worth troubling over. Still, with its many windows and spare lines the place must have been very attractive in its early years, before the plaster walls warped and the floorboards turned rheumatic, before the chimneys were sealed up forever, and the sloppy addition of indoor plumbing sent pipes coursing outside the walls. In the few old photos that still exist, the house has a wraparound porch, long gone, that gave it an airy hospitality. In one photo the Collins clan has gathered on the porch and front lawn, wearing the solemn expressions of slow exposure. My teenaged father is staring out from the saddle of a horse, wearing a haughty look, as if he were the lord of the manor.

In these prewar years Dad's family was reasonably comfortable, but far from affluent. They weathered the Depression partly by not having much to lose, and partly because both parents worked and were ingenious at making do. (My grandmother, for example, never stopped making her disgusting slimy soap mixture to use up the bits of spent bars.) Hoboes used to leave a mark near the house at 101 Pine Orchard Road, to let their brethren know they'd be welcome for a meal cooked by Alice Collins, invariably featuring fresh vegetables from her husband's garden.

America's middle class would not rise until after World War II, and in this poorer time expectations were lower. Dad's close-knit family of four rarely strayed far from Branford's simple, reliable pleasures, except to visit relatives in Massachusetts and New York. Moving to the big Collins spread with its generous acreage must have meant a proud step up to Alice Collins, a lover of good things who dressed her two children in fussy fine garments and posed them with the best furniture when their portraits were taken.

My Dad absorbed his mother's high expectations. He began to fulfill them by getting accepted to Yale College in nearby New Haven, after graduating with good grades from Branford High and acquiring a reputation for high ambition that would later mock him. With the blind brashness of youth, Jerry aimed for the top when he enlisted in the Marines—perhaps an ill-considered choice for a gangly, uncoordinated kid who trembled at the sight of blood.

At twenty years old, Dad had nearly completed Yale's accelerated wartime program when the messenger came to 101 Pine Orchard in June 1943, with the telegram notifying him he would soon be off to boot camp.

For my father, this telegram was like the pistol shot signaling the start of an Olympic footrace. It was time for Jerry Collins to go out on his own and prove he could measure up. That's why he'd enlisted in the Marines, after all: they were the toughest fighting unit in the world. When Jerry enlisted back in November 1942, the Marines were already burnishing their reputation for ferocious warfare, enhancing their appeal to countless thousands of young American heroes in waiting. If the green college boy felt a warning stab of dismay when he hit the notorious proving ground of Parris Island, a flea-bitten godforsaken patch fifty miles south of Charleston, South Carolina, he hid it well in his letters home.

Dear Mom and Dad:
I have to be brief because I haven't much time. So far so good. I like it here very much but also it is very tough, which I know it

has to be. Everything is discipline, but it's easy to get used to. I miss you all but nevertheless am glad I was called....

(Jerry's first letter from boot camp, July 16, 1943)

Dear Folks,

I've just had noonday chow and we have a little free time in our barracks.... So far all is okay with me except for this terrible heat. We wear fatigue clothes and sun helmets all the time and our khaki uniforms for special occasions.... I'm a squad leader, which means a lot of headaches for me when our squad has its work to do. We see a newspaper about every day. 3 or 4 papers to 67 men or so. We've got our rifles now and will probably be drilling with them soon. After 18 more or less days we go to the rifle range....

(July 21)

Dear Family,

Have just finished cleaning my rifle after a really tough drill on the field.... I would appreciate it if once a week you would send me a few cookies, etc. You know me at 10 pm or so.... How is Brownie? I wrote to Uncle Den and Aunt Nellie and will write to Grandma soon....

(July 23)

Dear Folks,

Today, for a change, is a day of rest, so I'm taking this chance to write to you. Yesterday we had typhoid shots and today we have sore arms.... Does Dad have to work often on Sundays? I hope not because it must be hot there now. I suppose you're eating carrots and squash every day now. I hope Brownie is behaving himself and that you haven't received any more complaints.... We're playing a double header this afternoon and the Sarge says win—or else. He's never had one of his platoons defeated so you can see what we're in for if we lose. I'll let you know the results.... We have to warm up for the game so for now I'll say so long. All of you keep writing and tell Sis to give me some news about Branford....

(July 25)

Dear family,
I had guard duty again last night and am I tired! Also hungry but no one has any food tonight.... Thursday is another inspection day and tomorrow is a big parade so I'll have to be on the ball. I dozed off at a lecture this afternoon and the DI had a pail of water placed behind him in case I fell off again. I didn't!!... I'm beginning to feel like a veteran here now. We have some new recruits below us, which makes us feel pretty seasoned.... Love to you all except Friskie [the family cat], Jerry

(August 3, 1943)

Dear Folks,
Today we fired machine guns and I shot high score in my group of 18 men.... Several fellows passed out from the heat today in our platoon and the ambulances have been very busy. I haven't had any trouble at all, except of course prickly heat, etc., which everyone gets. I'm as hard as a rock! Tomorrow we throw hand grenades for qualification.... You can have the army and Navy; I'll take the Marines. It's not possible that they give the training we get here. Marines are the best soldiers in the world and a qualified rifleman can shoot a soldier dizzy. Give my love to all....

(August 17)

Dear Folks,

…Guess what? As I was coming home from Church today who should I run into but Billy Clancy. He had just arrived at the range last night and lives about 2 minutes' walk from me. I'm going to meet him this afternoon and talk over the good old days. It's really good to see someone you knew before you came here.…

(August 22)

Dear Folksies:

Our DI has gone to breakfast so we have his radio on full blast listening to some enchanting Benny Goodman and Freddy Slack—simply bewitching. At present, the golden strains of "Cow-Cow Boogie" are floating through the barracks.

(August 25)

Week by week Jerry cheerfully reported home how the drill instructors "break their necks trying to make Marines out of us playboys." Along with his humbling chores of mending, washing, bed-making, and toilet-scouring—"Will I make a good wife!!"—my father was learning how to fieldstrip and reassemble at lightning speed his "piece," an M-I thirty cal. He was also mastering the particulars of firing on the rifle range, including positions, sling, and sighting, and the subtle science of "windage," or gauging the wind at various shooting distances to make allowances for its effect. "Out here on the range we work like animals and we all act like animals," he wrote in mid-August, just one month after leaving Branford. "Now I know what a dog's life is."

But he was proud of all his new skills, and seemingly oblivious of their ultimate purpose. He even had a buddy photograph him demonstrating each of the firing positions. The youngest platoon member also excelled at machine-gun firing and hand-grenade practice, and boasted how his platoon fielded the winning baseball team on Parris Island. He started sprinkling his missives with Marine lingo: "slop chute," "scuttlebutt," "dope," "skivvies," and other words he defined for his ignorant kin. Gradually Jerry grew confident in his regimented routine, enjoying the camaraderie of buddies who were all in the same boat, heading toward a war that still seemed remote and unreal.

This sensitive, physically soft boy, who'd never been away from home for more than a few days in his life, proved far more durable than his appearance had implied. He tanned and toughened under the harsh Carolina sun till his mother wrote with concern that she no longer recognized the rough creature in the photos.

But if outwardly my gentle father was transforming into that fiercest of warriors, the US Marine, underneath he was still a small-town kid missing the comforts of home. A bottomless pit, Jerry the notorious "icebox raider" sneaked off to the PX for ice cream every chance he got and cajoled his family to ship him some "pogey bait"—salted nuts, candy, and especially his mother's homemade cookies. "Oh for a homemade brew!" he pined.

Affectionately prodding "Maw, Paw, and Li'l Alice" to keep their letters coming, he loosed his own postal blizzard scrawled on plain paper or United States Marine stationery, asking for news of various Branford folks and Collins relations and regularly mentioning a girl named Edith. He speculated on when he'd qualify for a seventy-two or forty-eight-hour furlough; urged his dad to catch the Yale games and report on all their favorite sports teams; reassured his mother that he attended church each Sunday; and wrote that he hoped his "brother" Brownie, the cocker spaniel, had convinced their parents to send poor Jerry more spending "cabbage." The tone of his letters, startlingly strange to his own daughter decades later, was always lively and optimistic. He was deeply engaged in the doings back at 101 Pine Orchard, from the purchase of the latest family "chariot," a Ford Model A, to his "Glamour Girl" sister's latest beau. He particularly liked to tease his rather hoity-toity mother about her musical gifts: "So Brownie is still vocalizing. I always said he had the best trained voice in the family." In a letter to the cocker spaniel he wrote, "I noticed when I was home that you and mother had worked out a few lovely duets. Give Friskie a good bite for me, your brother Jerry."

The weeks of grinding, ego-busting routine wore on into August, till the toughest trial of boot camp finally arrived: Record Day on the rifle range. Snapping in and out of position on the blazing sand, the recruits had to shoot above a certain score or go home in shame, abandoning all hope to wear the Marine emblem of eagle, fouled anchor, and globe. "Eureka!" Jerry wrote home. "I qualified. I feel like a newly released prisoner." The next stop for this freshly anointed "rough tough master of sudden death": the Marine Corps' Officer Candidate School in Quantico, Virginia.

CHAPTER THREE

DAD'S BIG PLANS

Wedding photo of Jerry Collins and Blanche Ona Gutfinski

From the halls of Montezuma,
To the shores of Tripoli,
We fight our country's battles
On the land as on the sea.
First to fight for right and freedom
And to keep our honor clean;
We are proud to claim the title of
United States Marine.

("The Marines' Hymn")

On September 10, 1943, the newly minted Marine with his Private First Class stripes arrived at the imposing complex of Quantico in Virginia. "I feel honored to be here," Jerry wrote his parents, awed by the spectacle of full Marine regalia. The flood of new lieutenants set the OCS candidates saluting right and left, sparking their impatience to move up the ranks. "Wait till you see me in my snazzy officer's uniforms!" he wrote his sister Alice, drawing a cartoon of the clunky work boots he'd finally trade in for dress shoes once he earned his commission. So impressed was he by the snappy salutes and glossy privileges of rank, this dazzled PFC didn't register that he'd kissed his civilian autonomy goodbye and become one dog-tag number among countless others on the military assembly line moving toward war.

After the scorching ordeal of Parris Island, Jerry threw himself into the OCS regimen with cheerful enthusiasm. This was more like it: better food and classroom studies a Yalie could sink his teeth into. Here the candidates received more respect than the freshly shorn recruits at PI did. Their training broadened to include military tactics, map reading, field problems, and frequent three-day "wars" dubbed "the Battle of Quantico." Jerry reported regularly on his progress, proud of his good grades. Although he had arrived a lowly PFC he intended to depart an officer attracting his own flurry of salutes: "It won't be long before I can trade my stripe for a gold bar and my $54 a month for $150 a month," he declared.

Then came a setback: in October he landed in the hospital with a foot infection and missed some crucial days of testing. With the Pacific war heating up the Marines needed hordes of enlisted men, not officers. So Jerry Collins was out after barely more than a month, along with many other equally shocked and chagrined "washouts." This was the first big failure in my father's life and it took him completely by surprise. Refusing to surrender to "the blues," however, the OCS reject gamely downplayed his disappointment, gave himself and his parents pep talks, and went right back to making plans. He decided to stick with the Marines, hoping for advancement later on.

It seems as though the Marine Corps brass didn't know what to do with high-caliber flunkouts like my father, considered too intelligent, apparently, to send straight into the meat grinder. He tried to apply for training as a specialist in the new, up-and-coming radar technology, but there was too much red tape. In January he excitedly informed his parents he'd been selected for a special platoon that would undergo a new type of jungle warfare training, led by a famous Marine officer. That experience turned out to be a bust, dashing his hopes again. Then in February he was ordered to Camp Ritchie in Maryland for two months of "hush-hush" training in a combat intelligence and reconnaissance unit of fifteen men, chosen from all over the country. Being part of an elite Marine cell in an "army dogface" camp boosted his morale again: "the doggies certainly respect we 15 of God's chosen and clear a path for us in the P/X and slop shoot [sic]," he bragged. If he noticed the guinea-pig purpose of stray Marines like him, he didn't let on. He was hell-bent on winning a challenging assignment and a chance to prove his mettle.

After Camp Ritchie, Jerry was ordered in April to Camp LeJeune in North Carolina, where he joined the Second Battalion, Twenty-ninth Regiment of the newly formed Sixth Marine Division. "Boy, the way they talk about the 29th Marines all over the Post, I guess it's going to be about the best unit ever sent out," he reported proudly, signing off "your loving Marine."

In June Jerry finally landed his official assignment: the regimental intelligence section of the Second Battalion. This ragtag band of smart-alecky youths, most of them college educated, many of them OCS rejects just like Jerry, were the men with whom he would fight in the Pacific. Often, other Leathernecks goodnaturedly mocked them as "the college boys." Years later, one of their own, William Manchester, would immortalize the outfit in his war memoir as the "Raggedy-Ass Marines."

As training intensified Jerry's typical daily routine involved stalking, climbing, creeping, hiding, burrowing, crawling, and running for hours through a combat course in the North Carolina woods. When he wasn't tramping through the boonies on overnight exercises with his fellow "intelligence men," he managed to squeeze in letters to his family. His tone was consistently upbeat. Soon he would be traveling west to California, to board a troopship and leave the United States for the first time in his life. He couldn't wait to go.

Dear Alice,
The next time you see me will be when I return from overseas, which will probably not be until the war is over. So until then take care of yourself and help the folks out as much as you can to keep them happy....Keep things lively around the house and pick up a few zoot suits for me for when I go back to college.

(July 9, 1944)

Dear Folks,

I'm well on the way to California. We are riding in troop sleepers, which isn't bad at all. I'm seeing plenty of the USA anyway.... The railroad is treating us swell and the food is good. All my love Jerry

(July 18)

Dear Folks,

Today being Sunday I went to Mass, which was held up on the main deck. It was quite impressive to see all these Marines kneeling before God out in the middle of the great ocean aboard a ship which was a mere speck in a huge sea. We all know our destination and many of us had guessed it long ago.... I guess you don't realize how much you want the war to end until you leave the United States where it is so easy to forget about war or any unpleasant thing. I'm not complaining, however, as I have been through nothing and so many have sacrificed so much.

(August 6 aboard the troopship G. C. Morton *heading to Guadalcanal)*

I have been across the equator. We received the usual initiation by King Neptune, which consisted of a thorough paddling, a weird haircut, a dunking, a few good shots of electricity, and more paddling. So now I'm known as a "shell-back," and when I get my certificate I'll send it on home. Before your first trip across the equator you are known as a pollywog, which is as low as you can be.... I will close with all my love and will write every chance I get. The pride of the Marine Corps, Jerry

(August 20, still aboard)

When I was in my twenties, fresh out of college and marooned in Branford for the summer, my father told me for the first time what happened at Quantico. He put his OCS disappointment simply: "I washed out." It didn't seem to bother him at all, in retrospect anyway. In the end more than half of his fellow candidates didn't make the cut, including star athletes. So Dad was in good company. In fact, he dismissed the notion of ordering other Marines around. "I was better off sticking with my buddies," he said. "It was the enlisted men who did the heavy lifting in that war. There were a few good officers but most of them—" he shook his head with a familiar mix of pride and disgust, so proud to have been a workingman Leatherneck that one would think he'd have shunned a commission if it were offered.

Truth be told, while young Jerry Collins saw himself hardening into officer material the decision makers at Quantico probably observed something else. Most likely it was Dad's sensitive personality and lack of warriorlike traits that got him tossed. Ultimately, what the Marines sought in their leaders were not necessarily qualities my tender-hearted father possessed, no matter how hard he tried to act the role. Eventually I would learn from other World War II veterans who likewise washed out that their failure at Quantico haunted and depressed them throughout the war and, for some, forever after. Surviving boot camp only to be passed over at OCS for many Marines raised a host of self-doubts.

Would life have gone differently for Dad or for his family if he had made officer and gone through the war with that notch in his belt? Or, as a couple of his fellow vets have suggested, would he have been among the fledgling lieutenants shipped to Iwo Jima, where Japanese snipers easily targeted the inexperienced officers? In that case, Dad's failure may have saved his life. Nonetheless it was excruciating to learn from his own pen after his death that he once cherished exuberant aspirations and imagined himself a potential leader among men, a hero in the making.

If I look as far back as I can, I catch the last shimmer of those high-flying hopes. In my early childhood Dad was still making big plans, still expecting the pieces to fall into place. And in my mother he found his match in starry-eyed expectations.

The youngest of eight surviving children in a Polish immigrant family, Blanche Ona Gutfinski grew up in Hatfield in western Massachusetts, an old farming community where she spoke Polish and English at school and Polish and Latin at the Polish-Catholic church.

In his wedding day photograph my grandfather, *Dzazhiu* in Polish, is a strapping fellow with a feral gleam in his eyes and a spectacular mustache preparing for liftoff. The handsome peasant towers a foot above his tiny bride Antonia, my future *Bobki*, plump and solemn in her ornate gown decorated with sprigs of rosemary according to Polish custom. It was shy-looking Bobki who would rule the Gutfinski household with her daunting work ethic and stern Catholicism. Her husband was a dreamer and a drinker who spent a great deal of time in a shed behind the house, sipping homemade dandelion wine and entertaining young relatives with his naturalist interests.

The Depression hit my mother's newcomer family harder than my father's, and the Gutfinskis had to squeeze paying boarders in among their large brood. The local cash crops were onion and tobacco, with the hard-pressed farming families sharing labor, produce from their kitchen gardens, and a communal cow and chickens. All Gutfinski children performed a hefty share of manual labor. Blanche's enormous, capable hands were never free of calluses. After school and during summers she picked onions alongside other Gutfinskis, convicts from the local prison, and migrant workers. In 1937 the *Boston Globe* ran a story about Andrew Gutfinski's farm with a photograph of teenaged Blanche, her hair in a babushka, smiling into the camera as she worked in the fields with her elderly father, then in his seventies.

In 1943, as Jerry finished another semester at Yale and awaited his call to boot camp, Blanche was graduating from Massachusetts State College, her tuition paid by her generous older siblings. At Mass State the veteran field hand had happily changed her stripes and style to become a sorority sister and English major, class secretary for three years, and a member of the Honor Council. Blanche had dreams of European travel before going to work, but the war put them on hold—forever, it turned out. After teaching in Kittery, Maine, and Flint, Michigan, she took a job closer to home, at Branford High, and started making friends.

This sharp-witted, sociable girl with her hearty cackle of a laugh, olive green eyes, and dark Rosalind Russell mane caught the eye of Jerry Collins, newly returned from his tour of duty. They met at the Montowese House, the "Queen of the Sound," a grand hotel built in 1866 where Blanche waited tables in the public dining room during her summer off from teaching. Husky voiced, with a hint of a Polish accent, Blanche had an engaging radiance that had attracted many admirers, including a Jewish naval officer who devastated her when he wouldn't consider marriage, fearing his family's disapproval. In Jerry she found a good-looking, well-spoken Ivy Leaguer full of big plans and boyish charm who was determined to win her heart. It didn't hurt that he was Catholic, too. If his exuberant scheming occasionally smacked of wishful thinking, my smitten mother never took note.

She was already naively impressed by the wealth and standing of Jerry's family compared to hers. In fact, only the Irish patriarch Michael Collins had improved the family's fortunes, establishing wealth based entirely in a hefty chunk of Branford plus a few houses and, for a while, partnership in a popular local seafood emporium. Michael's son Jeremiah, Dad's father, was a diligent worker but no businessman; hard economic times apparently forced him out of his hardware store and into a wartime factory job making rifles. By the time Corporal Collins returned from the war another piece of family real estate was on the block—the fields where young Jerry once posed with Maisie the goat—and eventually became Collins Drive, a bland strip packed with early fifties houses. Shortsightedness would gradually whittle away the rest of Michael's land.

After a yearlong courtship Jerry and Blanche married on June 23, 1948, and moved to New Jersey, where he had lined up a good job as an industrial chemist for a chemical corporation. Somewhere along the way he'd abandoned his precious graduate school plans in favor of an immediate salary. But whether because of discontent, homesickness, or something more ominous, Jerry soon quit his job and convinced Blanche to move back to Branford. There they set up house and awaited their first child in another Collins property, the sweet white bungalow with stone pillars to the right of his parents' house on Pine Orchard Road. To the left of the old homestead stood a third Collins house where Jerry's sister Alice lived with her husband Bill Sadowski and their growing family.

Blanche set out to become the ideal homemaker while Jerry started a new career as a salesman, a postwar profession that promised the moon to confident and personable fellows like him. Every two years a baby boy arrived, first Jeremiah "Chippy" then Patrick "Ricky," and finally Peter. The side-by-side households became tightly entwined, with the senior Collinses presiding. Even though Jerry went through a string of sales jobs, never quite successful or satisfied in any one, and money was always tight, the family thrived. Nobody doubted that Jerry's fortunes would flourish once he found the right sales niche. He was the biggest believer of all— determined to claim his share of the American prosperity he had helped to secure in the war.

It would be hard to paint a rosier family portrait than that of the young Collins family during the decade before I came along: the clannish socializing from house to house, cousin sleepovers, raucous holiday gatherings, winter skating and sledding, summertime picnics with family and neighbors. My oldest brother recalls Kennedy-style Collins vs. Sadowski touch football games, Dad putting on a scavenger hunt for neighborhood kids, Uncle Bill and Dad singing "That's Amore" in drag at a church function, road trips in the station wagon to visit Gutfinski relatives in Hatfield, Gutfinskis arriving en masse in Branford for weekend visits. Back then Jerry Collins was full of fun when he wasn't racking up the miles pursuing a paycheck, and Blanche Collins was a cheerful, doting mother with no regrets over giving up teaching, which she'd been very good at, to preside over her own home. "Hello little white house, we missed you," she said fondly, whenever the Collins car pulled in front of the bungalow after some family trip.

But if asked, my brothers recall warning signs of the coming "Time of Troubles." As they grew older it became clear that Dad couldn't find his footing in the postwar boom. Every new opportunity he talked up, every prospect for big commissions proved a mirage. After years of slogging in his so-called gold-mine profession he still couldn't make enough money to support his family. His wife yearned passionately for the affluent home life of women's magazines, and compared her circumstances to those of her older married sisters, all of whom were prospering, buying new homes, and taking trips abroad. Jerry had not kept his word, and her patience thinned. When my grandfather Pop, beloved by all, died suddenly from a massive heart attack, a secret and essential source of assistance dried up, and a kindly, protective force in the family was gone. Frightened by her new widow status, my grandmother Angy decided to sell the bungalow to plump up her bank account. With nowhere else to go, Jerry moved his growing family into the homestead next door, just months after I was born.

After three boys and a gap of six years, I was a surprise. My youngest brother Peter had set his heart on another brother and had a name ready. To placate him, my parents brought home a rabbit and he became Richard while I became Julia Mary. Two years later my sister Jennifer, the fifth and last child arrived. The cramped, old-fashioned rooms of 101 PO could barely contain us all. My mother took on the lion's share of domestic duties and mourned the loss of her beloved bungalow across the way, chafing at her limited freedoms and authority as the junior Mrs. Collins on the premises.

By the time I was toddling around, a frowning child with dark eyes and blond wisps, my discontented mother began to enjoy the convivial sipping of the cocktail hour too much. Dad had grown up sampling his parents' homemade brews and, as a Marine, he often tossed down a six-pack or much more if the opportunity arose. Mom later swore to me that she never had more than a sip of alcohol until she became a Collins and started imbibing regularly at her in-laws' cocktail hours and neighborhood revels. My parents both gradually increased their intake of gin, bourbon, and vodka, fitting in comfortably with the hard-drinking style of the era. But it was Mom who developed an unquenchable thirst that made her edgy and nervous.

My father's behavior began to change too, not only from hitting the booze. His face would go blank as if he had checked out for a while, or freeze into an aloof and disapproving mask, or twist with inexplicable anger. He raised his voice more often with my brothers, especially Peter, fearing their judgment, even scorn, as they matured and measured him. He still cuddled with my sister, who was an adorable beaming elf; but at five years old I unnerved him because I was a moody worrier, nicknamed "Stormcloud," the same name as my rocking horse, for my dark moments and "Serenity" for when I lightened up again. The person he really began to steer clear of, though, was his wife. Drinking sharpened her tongue, brought out the bitterness. She started harping on fourteen years of unmet expectations.

The Collins family had food and a home thanks to our grandmother, but no medical or dental care. Our clothes were worn and patched. Although we certainly weren't poster kids for CARE, in 1960s go-go America, in our prospering town, my family's circumstances stood us out as weird, anomalous, mystifying, especially given my father's brains and seeming determination. I would have been oblivious to how poor we were becoming if not for the sense of fear and uncertainty emanating from my parents. I sometimes lay awake in my bed listening to them arguing downstairs, Mom's anguished voice rising sharply, Dad's droning wearily. Angy was blind to her son's struggles and too focused on her own priorities to pay much heed to the state of his family, but one time I heard her imperiously command my parents to work out their differences quietly. "You're behaving disgracefully," she snapped.

Even I, with my baby teeth and lingering lisp, felt trouble brewing. With three kids Mom and Dad had managed, barely, but with four and then five, they were in over their heads. Though I'm certain Mom never thought so, I suspect my father did. And because I saw myself as a burden, I worked extra hard to be a good girl, to make him love me. Unfortunately, I was not a charming child, with my weight-of-the-world demeanor. I could tell when Dad began to pull away from me for good—though I would still prove a useful listener.

When the tension inside 101 PO grew unbearable, I escaped outdoors. In Branford a child could vanish for hours with no one raising an alarm. In our backyard, to the left near the old apple tree was a pockmarked, overgrown patch the boys had made into foxholes back when they played at war. To the right was the sledding hill, a fine ride if one swerved clear of the cesspool overflow down at the bottom. The fields were gone now, but at the back of the house where the sun set the woods began, thickening behind a whale's back of gray stone atop which lay a massive boulder we called the Indian Prayer Rock. Eventually the woods ran out at the Sand Pit where a huge bite out of the land had left behind an enthralling lunar landscape of rocky mounds, swampy patches we called quicksand, and stands of scraggly trees. Miff and I mostly stuck close to home, making our puddle soups, picking ragged bouquets, climbing the cherry tree, digging in the dirt, following our mother around, but our big brothers, two of them already in their teens, wandered far and wide.

Our neighborhood was packed with kids back then, most of them living on Collins Drive. Of the several little girls on the street, I passed over the sweet ones to choose sassy Stacey Ketchum as my particular friend. She had a smart-mouthed derring-do that attracted me. We were both in Miss Chadwick's kindergarten class and I was awed by Stacey's precocious passion for another five year old named Stevie. Stacey was into kissing: how she would kiss Stevie, when, and where. I had a beau too, named Hugh, but our relationship didn't go much beyond him fetching my little glass bottle of milk at snack time every day and stammering when I thanked him.

As Mom and Dad bickered and lost sight of their children, we were forced to become more self-sufficient. We figured out that it was up to us to preserve family harmony by staying out of the way and causing no trouble to anyone, especially our distracted parents. All five of us were remarkably well behaved and eager to please, painfully alert to any shift in the barometric readings of 101 PO.

I realized for the first time that I was on my own when my training wheels became an intolerable humiliation. Because of a malformed ear, caused by rubella Mom contracted when I was in her womb, I had terrible balance that gave me trouble when it came to bicycling or skating or gymnastics. Miff was already cruising on the two-wheeler we shared while I keeled over after only a few yards whenever Dad took off the training wheels. He finally lost patience with picking me up and patching my scrapes. "You're on your own, kiddo," he sighed.

I stewed for a while in helpless shame and despair. Then one morning I got up so early even my parents were still in bed. I could barely see to throw on my clothes. The day was so fresh it hadn't picked out its colors yet. Everything was shadowy, except for a splash of pink to the east. I removed the banged-up training wheels and quick-marched the bike to the smooth tar of Collins Drive, my heart thumping wildly. There were no cars on the road. The drab boxy houses were sleeping, except for a light here and there. I gritted my teeth and for the next hour I got on the bike, pedaled furiously, fell down, got on again, fell down, and got on again. The handlebars were slick with sweat, my legs covered in bleeding scratches when the glorious moment finally arrived: all at once I found my elusive center of gravity and pumped as fast as I could. I rode to the end of the street and turned in a swooping arc, passing Mrs. Mickelson who waved and called good morning. I couldn't answer because I had started to cry, my whole body quivering with elation and misery. After a few more loops I rode home, parked the bike, and went inside to soothe my cuts with a cold washcloth, hiding them under long pants. Nobody knew that I'd been gone, and nobody noticed later on that I was no longer using training wheels. It hurt my feelings for a brief while, as if my birthday had passed without anybody saying a word, but then I realized with a thrill that I was becoming like my brothers. Like them, I had a secret life my parents knew nothing about.

All at once the ominous weather pattern at home cleared and brightened. Perhaps Angy intervened with an ultimatum or perhaps my parents scared themselves because they rallied for a while. Mom's drinking subsided. She rose each day miraculously regenerated, eager to pounce on a thousand tasks. "Brighten the corner where you are," she sang in her hoarse, erratic alto as she waved the feather duster around, a determined Pollyanna in a well-worn dress.

As for Dad, his paychecks became more reliable. Then he scored his first solid sales job and began jetting all over the country demonstrating cryosurgical equipment to major hospitals. He got a kick out of staying in nice hotel rooms and eating fancy restaurant meals. He brought home a plastic treasure chest filled with fake beads from Mardi Gras in New Orleans and other booty from distant parts. He regaled us with his on-the-road escapades—befriending a cabbie who took him on a late-night tour of San Francisco when he had insomnia, tussling with a pickpocket in Houston, taking a fieldtrip to the Chicago slaughterhouses to pick up a plastic drum filled with pig eyes, which he used to demonstrate his wares.

Dad took pride in his amateur surgical prowess. One night he made the mistake of telling me he sometimes operated on rabbits, too. When I got upset at the idea of bunnies going under his knife and asked what happened to them afterward, a funny look came over Dad's face and he started to weep. I stood in frozen panic, waiting for the dark mood gripping my father to go away. "A bad memory," he finally explained.

As his fortunes briefly rose, Dad entertained the notion of running for the office of first selectman of our town. Years later he told me some townsmen had asked him to run; I'd like to think that was so. Nothing came of it, but he continued to follow local and national politics closely. A staunch populist Democrat, he was full of opinions about this crook or that dope or bozo running for office. On weekends he whistled as he puttered about the yard, read his papers and smoked, presided over the barbecue grill and the dinner table, attempted domestic repairs, and chauffered his wife, who had never learned to drive, on her errands about town. He and Mom even stepped out for the evening every now and then, usually to a party at one of the neighbor's houses.

It filled me with wild hope to see them in their party clothes, to watch my father helping my mother into her swing coat, to feel her waxy red kiss goodnight. I can still picture us two little girls wearing our bootied winter jammies and gazing up at Mom and Dad, trusting in their ineffable adult powers. I knew my parents, in their early forties now, were no longer young. They were older than all my friends' parents. I'd begun to worry that someday my mom and dad would die. But when I watched her pat his cheek, and saw him grip her hand, smiling, my fears disappeared for a while.

While we no longer did much as a family, on Sunday mornings the Collinses all dressed up and set off for mass in two cars. As soon as we got to St. Mary's my brother Peter helped Angy maneuver the steep ascent to the organ loft, where a magnificent rose window illuminated her perfectly manicured hands as she deftly flicked stops and attacked the keys. Her elderly but sure soprano soared over the congregation, causing heads to turn and search for the source.

Our church was a gilded cavern supported by massive columns, the gloom pierced by medieval-looking lanterns and the beams of light streaming in through the stained glass. Everywhere one glanced were unblinking martyrs, scenes of Christ's suffering, warnings of the Judgment Day to come. To occupy us during the long service my mother handed me and Miff each a notepad and pencil. Sometimes I scribbled questions and Mom wrote answers. Does God have a last name? *No.* Was Jesus his only child? *Yes.* Why did God let him die? *I'll explain later.* Did Jesus have a wife? *No.* Why not? *I'll tell you later.* I'm hungry. What's for dinner? *Pot roast corn and bo-day-does.* I love you Mommy. *I love you Julie. Now listen to Father Healy.* Meanwhile my father stared at the altar, poker-faced, obviously bored but performing his part as head of the family. His presence inspired me on one occasion to draw a wild-haired Jesus jumping out of the tomb with a rifle, an M-1, of course, to shoot all of those rotten Romans who crucified him. My mother looked down, saw my handiwork, plucked off the piece of paper and slid it into her purse so nobody in the pew behind us would see.

I gradually outgrew my doodling and began to pay attention to the mass. Soon I was praying in earnest, channeling all my prayers toward one futile goal. "Dear God, keep Mommy and Daddy happy," I pleaded, knotting my fingers together till they ached. "And please, help Daddy earn more money." I begged God so hard my head hurt. When mass ended and my grandmother's thundering organ swept us through the heavy portals, I emerged into the daylight and waited for God to take action.

Our weekly habit was to stop in Dunbar's Pharmacy after mass for candy and comic books and sometimes Castellon's Bakery for Hummel hot dogs and rolls for lunch. When we got home my spirits were racing from sugar and I waited happily for divine intervention, a signal from God to me, Julie Collins, his loyal supplicant, that things were going to be A-OK. Inevitably I began to crash from the sugar and saw nothing had changed. Our house looked pathetic. The worn linoleum, the hole in the playroom wall nobody bothered to fix, the sweating icebox on its last legs, the leaky pipes and tattered upholstery that made my mother so disconsolate would never go away. And we were the same too, acting the way we always did: Dad slipping outdoors to smoke alone; Mom tight-lipped as she set about making lunch, her noisy movements expressing discontent; Angy disappearing into her room to listen to opera on the radio; and all of us kids keeping out of the way.

I was too young to record how long the truce lasted between my parents. But I know it ended abruptly. One night in late spring, after Dad and Mom had a fight about money and she slapped his face, he stood in the driveway smoking, his face drawn and remote. I went out to him hesitantly. I had found out earlier, from one of my brothers, that he had lost his great job. Later Mom would claim he was fired because he couldn't make his quota, and he would insist he fell behind in sales because her drinking kept him off the road to look after us kids. Usually I suspected my father was in the wrong, but my mother was undeniably changing before our eyes, turning volatile and caustic.

Dad smiled when he saw me coming, dropped his cigarette, crushed it under his loafer, and opened his arms. "Choolie," he said, picking me up and holding me to his chest. "Choolie-woolie, don't you worry about your mother and me. Everything is fine. I'm going to get a new job and money's going to start rolling in. Then I'll buy your mother and you and your sister and brothers anything you want. For starters, I'm going to give you kids fifty dollars apiece. How about that?!" His dark eyes glowed. I nodded, tightening my arms around his neck, pressing my cheek to his. I knew he was full of it, and my heart was breaking. My daddy was a lying bastard, just like I'd heard my mommy say. What would become of us?

Not long afterward, when he'd gotten a job selling insurance again, commission only, no salary, Dad let his hopes run away with him and he opened savings accounts for my sister and me at the Branford Savings Bank. Not for my brothers: he didn't bother trying to impress or win them over any more. The boys were too grown up and wise, too accustomed to him not living up to his word. For a month Dad regularly showed me my passbook, pointing out the weekly deposits. Then he stopped talking about my account, and I knew not to ask. After he died, I found two old passbooks in his file cabinet. I opened the one with my name on it: after making several ten-dollar deposits Dad had withdrawn all the money.

As I went from first grade to second, the fights escalated at home. Mom became oddly furtive; she disappeared for brief spells and came back a different person. Her temper alternated between exuberantly loving and disparaging. She found fault most with my father, but all of us seemed to inexplicably irritate and wound her. Dad's drinking worsened too. Most evenings his breath was a heavy cloud of hard liquor. I hated when he came up to say goodnight.

Our bedtime ritual became an ordeal. He sounded impatient when he sang, cutting off verses, forgetting his place. His ramblings grew more frightening and hard to follow. In the morning he woke in a testy mood and seemed eager to get out of the house, away from his wife and kids.

Far worse, he was acting too friendly with one of the neighbors, my best pal Stacey's mom, Mrs. Ketchum, a brunette bombshell with a dicey reputation. Much younger than my parents—I'd learned she had her first child at fifteen—in hot weather she lounged for hours in plain view, oiled and packed into a white bikini. Dad inevitably pushed the lawnmower in her direction. As I watched him wave to the woman Mom had started to call "that trollop," I sizzled inside with the wretched helpless anger only children experience. I didn't exactly understand what it meant when my father turned off the mower engine and stood there so impudently, chatting and joking with our pretty neighbor in full view of his family and hers. I was sure, however, that their flashing smiles were a factor in the intensifying conflict between my parents.

CHAPTER FOUR PEACE ON EARTH

The family home at 101 Pine Orchard Road in Branford, Connecticut

Dear Folks,

The longer I am away the more I realize what a wonderful family I have. You, Mother and Dad, sacrifice so much for us and receive so little in return. You sent me to one of the most expensive schools in the country and now you want me to return to graduate school....From now on I'm doing it myself with my own money and the [GI] Bill of Rights. I can picture that dinner which was always so good and my mouth waters. We are having turkey also, so don't worry about my Christmas. The Marine Corps usually comes through....

(On Guadalcanal, Christmas Day 1944)

When US Marines invaded Guadalcanal in the Solomon Islands and wiped out the Japanese occupying force after a ferocious engagement, "the Canal" became an American training ground for upcoming assaults leapfrogging toward Japan. In August 1944 the troopship ferrying PFC Jerry Collins from San Diego landed at the island, where for the next seven months his reconnaissance squad underwent rigorous training for an upcoming invasion—the target as yet unknown to the enlisted men.

Jerry was dazzled at first by the strange, unsettling lushness of Guadalcanal—the indolent palms bending toward the warm Pacific, the garishly plumed birds and parrots, the monstrous snakes and insects, the stupendous waterfalls and towering cliffs carved by rivers coursing across the interior. At night he looked for the Southern Cross decorating the unfamiliar night sky. Each morning he shook out his boondockers in case any of the army of loathsome, black-shelled land crabs had scuttled inside.

While he adapted to life on the Canal, Jerry wrote home pleading for snack foods, text books, and especially socks because his Marine allotment disintegrated quickly in the steamy climate. He teased his mother over her diet and her latest driving fiasco. He asked after his father's Victory Garden and reminisced about "charcoal specials" from the grill, adding, "I keep telling myself it can't be but I'm convinced we eat goat here."

His dad was now a defense worker at the Winchester rifle factory and his mom had an office job; he jokingly called her "the executive." In letters to his sister Jerry worried about his parents, especially their father's tendency to brood over the news, and urged her to make them "step out" more often. He also asked Alice, the prettiest girl in her class, to send a picture of herself to his buddy Les Penny in whom he took a special interest. "He's very good looking and full of fun," Jerry wrote, adding how Les, who lived with foster parents on a chicken farm, "has no mother or father and hasn't had much of a life." In one of her letters, Alice broke the news that Edith, her brother's Branford love interest, had gone and married someone else. He got over it quickly, however, for his pen pals included several women he'd met along the way since boot camp.

By late autumn Jerry had become a crack shot. His lean body was darkly tanned, his scouting skills sharp. Named chief observer, he liked the freedom that came with patrolling and detested the regiment's weekly inspections by rigid Colonel Victor Bleasdale, the "Silver Fox." Although he continued his diligent "plugging for that second stripe," Jerry was losing hope that his hard work would be rewarded with a promotion. His letters tartly reflected annoyance at an erratic process of advancement that skipped over many deserving men. The swashbuckling Marine Corps had also begun to lose some luster in his eyes for its innately undemocratic ways. "I can never understand why enlisted men are treated as inferior types of human beings with a next to nothing mentality," he wrote home. "Why, there are a lot of men in our section who could make the leaders look foolish in the field."

Unmerited privileges of rank frustrated him, as did the dull-witted ineptitude of certain officers. I later heard from Dad how some of his commanding officers were duped by a charismatic con artist named Red DeGreve into assigning him to the Twenty-ninth Regiment as a Japanese interpreter. Red, in fact, spoke not a word of Japanese. He taught an imaginative gibberish that his Marine students dutifully parroted until their instructor's bold lies and criminal record finally caught up with him—and he moved on to his next scam.

It was on Guadalcanal that the scrappy reconnaissance squad became a cohesive unit as Jerry and his comrades learned to trust and rely on one another despite their sundry upbringings—rich, poor, urban, rural, North, South, Christian, Jewish. Such distinctions seemed insignificant out in the middle of the Pacific Ocean. There were no black Leathernecks, however. Later my dad would wonder why the Marine Corps hadn't desegregated for the war. He insisted that even racial divisions would have been abandoned, as useless extra weight, for the sake of the fighting brotherhood.

Mutual tolerance was essential when living in close, uncomfortable quarters under constant stress. Sometimes the boys got on each other's nerves and gibing turned mean-spirited, occasionally cruel. Mostly, however, they came to appreciate one another's eccentricities and talents. A barbershop quartet formed—though Jerry didn't join, having grown up with a musically ambitious mother who had prodded him on stage too many times. He was more of an observer, relishing his new buddies' colorful characteristics—Stan the amateur hypnotist, John the jokester, Bill the aspiring writer, Mack the preacher, "Pop" the wise old man of the group at thirty, and so forth.

As training intensified, Jerry's unit frequently left the rest of the battalion behind to go on long scouting missions in the sweltering interior. "I'm turning into a mountain goat climbing all these hills," he wrote, "and as for coconuts I'll never care much for them anymore." In their free time he and his buddies swam, fished, studied, played sports, attended the occasional movie or USO show, and pulled pranks on their CO, an ineffectual and profoundly irritating lieutenant from the South they called 'Bama. Jerry spent hours listening to records on the mess hall Victrola with a sergeant buddy and tuned the radio nightly to Tokyo Rose for her enchanting music and sinister death wishes for the American troops so far from home. He devoured the twenty-five-cent mysteries and historical novels that dominated the Marine lending library. Upset at the prospect of losing ground in his college subjects, he was euphoric when he found out Yale had granted him a bachelor's degree even though he'd been called up one semester shy of graduation.

Throughout December the heat thickened and the sweating Marines grew restive. For Jerry, the island that had appeared paradisiacal at first blush revealed itself as a breeding ground for alarming critters and infections. Its jungles were an ensnaring tangle reeking of rot, its lagoons and swamps scummy. He extricated himself from leeches and stinging centipedes and fought off armies of mosquitoes. As the routines of the Canal wore on he began to drink more, using up his rations and donations from tee-totalling friends. "Our tent has quite a beer supply and today is our day, at least mine, to escape in mind from our island," he wrote to his parents, reflecting his altering mood and new maturity.

Scuttlebutt intensified about the looming engagement. Jerry sensed he and his buddies were heading for the vortex. The war was turning against the Japanese, but casualties on both sides were mounting with each successive fight. A million more deaths were projected once the conflict reached Japan's home islands. The men all knew this. With that in mind, Jerry countered rumors his parents must have passed on, that the fighting might end soon.

"It will be a long war, as we out here can tell," he insisted. For the first time, his letters indicated the divide between the fighting men and "you people" safe and ignorant on the home front.

Stuck in the Pacific tropics, with winter turned on its head, Jerry became sorely homesick as the holidays approached. He longed for his mother's cooking, deep snow, cold air, the smell of balsam, and the carefree revelry his little family so relished. On his first Christmas Eve away from home he dutifully reported that he had attended Midnight Mass and hid his moroseness. As the last days of 1944 ran out, his wistful thoughts kept circling back to his childhood and Branford, thousands of miles away.

On the cusp of 1945, Jerry Collins couldn't wait to get off Guadalcanal and into the real action—his goal since he'd first enlisted in November 1942. The coming year would prove the most climactic and ruinous of my father's life. When I was growing up, and Dad told me about his months on the Canal, I felt the grip of sadness even in his light-hearted accounts. The tedious months he spent on that remote island were his last peace on earth before the war swallowed him whole.

> I've been thinking of all the past years recalling things we used to do so often. Remember when Sis and I used to drag you to Savin Rock and how we always had to make a stop at Clark's Dairy for one of those immense sundaes with that whipped cream they used to pile on? I can still picture Dad in the old days clattering down the street with Ralph Linden and me hanging on throwing newspapers. I can even remember him teaching you how to drive and you would end up crying. And how happy I was to get my bicycle and the time Sis stepped on my uke. We used to drag you and Dad out of bed at 4 in the morning on Christmas. . . .
>
> (January 19, 1945)

* * *

In the 1960s a lot more snow seemed to fall on Connecticut, and Christmastime in Branford was the naive wonderland of sentimental greeting cards. I expect it looked pretty much the same in my time as it did in my dad's. Festooned in garlands and gussied up with holiday window displays, our stodgy Main Street briefly came to life. A Christmas tree and a large crèche appeared on the town green—Hanukkah candles would not join them for a while yet. Church ladies baked and knitted and sewed for the hectic round of holiday fairs. Choruses rehearsed the Messiah and carol sings all over town. Ponds cooperatively froze for skaters and Flexible Flyers took to the hills. Elementary school classes cranked out construction paper decorations, pipe-cleaner candy canes, and boxes coated in gilded macaroni. *A Charlie Brown Christmas* and *Rudolph the Red-Nosed Reindeer* made their annual TV appearances. Scraggly Santas rang bells and offered up their laps for good causes. With the energy crisis still in the future, houses lit up the night with exuberant blinking lights and glowing plastic figures of Jesus, Santa driving his sleigh, the Nutcracker, and Christmas carolers all celebrating together.

I remember one Branford holiday tradition in particular: the annual Christmas trolley ride for local kids. We clambered onto the antique cars with their butt-spanking seats and blurry windows, to shimmy off into the no man's land between our town and East Haven where the cars lived year-round in a museum. As they picked up speed we were whipped into holiday frenzy by a local phenomenon named Mrs. H, a hale and hearty bespectacled Viking with a high-rise braided hairdo who went from car to car pumping her gorgeous accordion and belting out carols in a booming, authoritative alto. I was always alarmed when she burst into my car, elbows akimbo, fingers flying as she exhorted us to apply our chirpy voices to "Joy to the World" or

"Hark the Herald Angels Sing," blithely leaving us behind on the unfamiliar verses. On this Christmas journey Mrs. H was the star of wonder, star of might, and Santa her lowly sidekick: he followed in her wake, mildly ho-ho-ing as he handed out mesh stockings filled with candies. I have no idea who I sat with from one year to the next, for the only two faces I recall are those of ruddy-cheeked Mrs. H and my watchful father standing by when the trolley cars pulled in.

Let me bring back my dad, the way he was when I was seven, just before I began to lose him for good. He stands motionless alongside the tracks, waiting for me to leap from one of the opening doors. His hair is glossy black like coal in the flat wintry light. His keen eyes flick from car to car, as tendrils of cigarette smoke and respiration curl from a long thin mouth like mine. It's a rare event to have the traveling salesman waiting just for me, and I'm already searching for him while the rest of the kids obediently wrap up the caroling and Mrs. H's accordion wheezes its last note. In the sudden silence the wheels squeal to a halt alongside the platform and there he is, the stiff posture and arrogantly up-tilted chin easy to spot. Even in the holiday throng he's the obvious loner, stationing himself apart from the other parents, not unfriendly yet somehow unconnected, a cautious observer guarding his thoughts. I bolt from my seat to be first off when the door finally opens, desperate to get to him, afraid of something happening before I do. Sure enough, even when he grins at the sight of me, lifts a hand and calls out something jolly and silly, I can tell he's distracted, eager to move on. I trot alongside him to the station wagon, sad because he doesn't take my hand anymore, the way he used to. He tells me to get in and wait while the engine warms up and he clears fresh snow off the windshield. He's scowling now, fussily swiping the brush across each window, a neatnik Virgo through and through. His cigarette burns down too close to his lip and he spits it onto the ground with an angry jerk of his chin. Then he's climbing in beside me, rubbing his gloveless hands together. My father underdresses for winter, never seems to own a decent overcoat, catches one cold after another. He snorts back some of his perpetual postnasal drip. He fastidiously checks the mirror, wipes off some fog. He sighs and frowns, clearly in a snit for some reason, maybe my fault for making him wait too long in the cold. By now I'm close to crying, wishing I hadn't gone on that ride. But suddenly my daddy pats my knee, aware of me again. "Hey now, duchess, how 'bout some of that candy for your chauffeur," he wheedles, his mood brightening before my eyes. Then we're both happily sucking sweets as the station wagon swings its loose, aging hips over the softly powdered streets. Once his hands are warm, my father finally asks me about my excursion: was it fun? Amused at the picture of Mrs. H and her accordion, he wants to know what songs we sang. So we loudly carol together the rest of the way home.

By the time of that particular trolley ride, 101 Pine Orchard Road had become an uneasy place of unpredictable outbursts, bitter looks between my parents, Mom's tears, Dad's shouting, my grandmother's staunch obliviousness. I think my brothers were old enough to guess what might be coming. Jennifer and I weren't, but we both had unknowingly begun to practice our roles in the battle shaping up. I grew warier and quiet, keeping an eye on everyone, and Miff became more insistently endearing, a desperate little disarmer.

Each Christmastime, however, Mom and Dad called a cease-fire, and we all relaxed in the temporary calm. I don't know how they pulled it off but they mostly succeeded, at least in the early years. Two sentimental souls, they loved holidays and joined forces to make Christmas special. They cut back on the booze and were nicer to each other. I catalogued every sign of affection I witnessed with satisfaction, as if my parents were wisely saving up in a joint account, guaranteeing the future of their marriage.

We Collinses were out of step in our middle-class community of rising incomes, second cars, and vacations to Hawaii or Yellowstone or New England lakes. Despite our decline into poverty, at holiday time my family became temporarily rich in traditions linking us to previous generations and another continent, reinforcing our place in the world, dispelling for a while our growing isolation.

No other home was as valiantly festive as ours was, thanks to my industrious mother. She set candleboards in the windows, brought out the holiday music and books, hung mistletoe, arranged poinsettias, and displayed Christmas gewgaws everywhere. Then she loaded a wheelbarrow with boughs she cut from our evergreens and turned out wreaths and swags, some for us, some for the dead Collinses at St. Agnes Cemetery. Her finest creation was the enormous wreath decorated with fake fruit, nuts, and berries and a giant bow that she hung out front. "You haven't mentioned my gorgeous Della Robbia yet," she pouted, if compliments came too slowly.

Angy and Mom kept our ancient kitchen stove going for hours on end, watchful and hovering because the blackened ovens were eager to burn. Together they stoked the family sweet tooth with their assembly-line output of candies, cookies, and pastry. Angy tied herself into a homemade apron and deployed an arsenal of arcane cooking gadgets. She pressed springerle dough into birds and wheat and flowers with a specially carved rolling pin and dipped iron forms in batter then hot oil to make crisp rosettes dusted with powdered sugar. I applied my puny force to the Rocket nutcracker to break open the giant pecans she ordered direct from Georgia for Creole pralines and tassies

baked in tiny tins. Mom's bailiwick was mass-producing gingerbread and sugar cookies from popular women's-rag recipes, for
which she deployed an army of ancient cookie cutters, some so
banged up that every camel had a pinched neck and the bells all
came out wobbly.

Fake trees were in vogue back then but we turned up our
noses and got ours from a local nursery. Dad was the expert,
using his height plus two hands' length to select the perfect fragrant specimen. Back at the house Miff and I went to work
stringing popcorn and cranberries while he tested the light
strings. Every night I sat on the stair landing opposite the tree,
lost in exalted meditation, mesmerized by the colored lights and
winking tinsel, a lump of anxiety weighing in my chest because I
felt the peaceful hours whipping past, propelling us toward tur-
moil and uncertainty.

On Christmas Eve I awoke in the dark to the faint music of
the sleigh bells my father shook so we would know the reindeer
were landing. He'd taken over this little ritual from my grandfather Pop, who had strolled jingling and jangling through the
neighborhood to thrill the wakeful children. Straining to hear
Santa at work downstairs, I lay awake in painful ecstasy. Come
morning, when we flew downstairs after daybreak, a mountain of
presents my parents couldn't afford would be waiting under the
tree, signed from Rudolph, Mrs. Claus, the Elves, Santa, the
Grinch. Mom would be busy in the kitchen beating sourdough
pancake batter while Dad smoked contentedly in the living
room, on the lookout for our reactions when we saw the tree
swamped in presents. In the hour before church time we reveled
in the annual Collins gift-giving frenzy, we children bestowing as
eagerly our parents, sparing no effort or expense relative to our
allowances or my brothers' after-school incomes. While we
always got a few extraordinary things, most of our gifts were

modest or practical items such as writing paper or mittens. The point wasn't how much the offerings cost but how easily we lavished them on this one idyllic day of unfettered abundance.

Although each December found us poorer, Mom and Dad shared a boundless, irresponsible generosity in defiance of all good sense. Medical care could be skimped on, new clothes and music lessons too—in fact we could do without just about anything except for our Christmas blowout. It particularly inspired a giddy, boyish largesse in Dad, who returned from sales trips with a car full of presents paid for on bad credit. Once I heard my mother complaining to him about the money he was spending, fretting over New Year's deprivations to come. She shut up the instant she realized I was nearby, afraid she'd given up the goods on Santa.

One year Dad was on the road right up until Christmas Eve. Mom grew more agitated by the hour, clearly anxious for him to come home. I didn't know it then but our holiday was in grave danger. There had been no money to buy any presents. My father hadn't gotten a paycheck in many weeks. For the first time ever, my parents were going to fail to deliver, a catastrophe in a family so dependent on its annual miracle.

Dad pulled in long after dinnertime, honking the horn as he turned the car around. Mom rushed out to meet him, and when they came in together he glowed with triumph. He'd gotten paid that afternoon but by then it was too late to do anything about Christmas. He made the long drive home in a state of dejection, dreading the prospect of a barren tree. On the way he nearly overlooked a lonely store in an unlikely location, miraculously lit up after all other shops had closed. It turned out to be a toy shop—in fact, the finest he'd ever been in—and he ran through his paycheck in an exhilarating buying spree. After crowing over his triumph, Dad abruptly buttoned up, remembering Miff and me. We got some malarkey about parents always giving

Santa a hand, which satisfied us. I was only too willing to believe—in Dad, Mom, Santa Claus, God, Rudolph the Red-Nosed Reindeer, whoever and whatever would keep us in this contented state.

Of course the annual truce between my parents couldn't endure. During our last Christmas season together I woke one night to a crashing sound. I came downstairs in time to see Mom prostrate on the floor by the darkened tree, unmistakably drunk, still clutching a bottle in her hand. Shards of broken plates were scattered about. My father towered over her, one hand squeezed into a fist. "THAT'S ENOUGH, BLANCHE," he snarled. Mom was too far gone to register my presence, but Dad turned and scowled at me. "Go back upstairs, Julie. RIGHT NOW."

As far as I know, everybody else was asleep. I lay in bed sniveling, curled up like a possum, the cold air of the unheated room boring a hole in my heart. I was sure I would die of misery. And I was ashamed of myself, though I didn't know why. There was something I ought to have done, or not have done, to help fix what was happening downstairs.

A while later my father appeared at my bedside, a somber silhouette. He sat on the mattress, leaning over me so he could whisper without waking Jennifer. He stroked my hair and apologized for scaring me. Mom was very sick, very sad, but she would get help, he said in his gentlest persuasive voice. Everything was going to be fine. I could tell his comfort was a lie. He and Mom would never be happy again. And I suspected that Mrs. Ketchum figured in this, somehow. He was a liar, just like Mom said. At the same time, she was losing control of her thirst, driving Dad away. I couldn't figure out which parent to blame more, or for what.

"You hit her," I whispered.

"I didn't want to, Julie. She came at me, waving a bottle. I wish it hadn't happened. I won't hit your mother ever again."

"Is she okay?"

"She's fine. She's sleeping now. Don't you worry, honey."

Then my father did something horrible. He tried to win me over. "Julie, you need to understand. Your mother isn't thinking straight these days. When she drinks she imagines things. All that crap she says about me and Mrs. Ketchum—"

I began to sob. He tried to soothe me but I turned my face into the pillow, rejecting his comfort. After a couple of minutes the mattress rose when he stood and left the room.

It took me a long time to fall asleep. My ecstatic Christmas hopes were replaced by nightmare images of my warring mom and dad. I have no memory of how the world appeared the next morning—whether my mother was sober, what my parents said to us kids, how they behaved toward each other, whether we celebrated Christmas as if nothing had happened. I do know that night I lost my unquestioning love for my father.

After my parents split up, Christmas changed for good. Dad was no longer Santa Claus. Kicked out of Mom's heart, demoted in our family, he was stripped of his bells, foolish with his empty sack. His job prospects worsened and my mother, forced to become the primary breadwinner, took over buying the Christmas presents. For a while she continued the game of signing "Merry Christmas from Frosty," "Greetings from the Elves," "Ho, ho, ho from Santa," but eventually the tags all said "Love, Mom." My father receded to the sidelines on Christmas mornings, accepting and opening the gifts presented to him, politely thanking but no longer part of the exchange.

During one of these bleak seasons, on a raw day in the last week of December, Dad drove me into town to exchange one of my gifts from Mom, a pair of corduroy pants. As we passed the cemetery on Montowese Street he made a terrible choking noise. I thought he was sick till I saw he was fighting back tears. I was an advanced eleven by then, full of angst and haughty judgments, and the sight of my dad breaking down was intolerable. Mom had practically ordered him to take me to Palaia's clothing store, make himself useful for God's sake, and I guessed that must have been the final straw. "Pull over," I begged, nervous he would lose control of the car. He did, and after a moment I asked carefully, "What's the matter, Dad?" It would have to do with Mom, surely, or all of us, how he had let us down.

"Nuttin', Chule," he said in a strained voice.

I sighed. "Come on, Dad. Now you have to tell me."

He surprised me: he wasn't thinking about Mom or us at all. He was thinking about Christmas, he said, but not in Branford and not in my lifetime. He was remembering Christmas on Guadalcanal, where he was stationed for months of jungle warfare training. It was the worst Christmas of his life—the first he'd ever spent away from his mother, father, and sister. He was afraid he wouldn't make it back, killed in the invasion all the boys knew was imminent. Or, that if he did survive and return to Branford in one piece, nothing would be the same. He broke down in front of me, all these years later, because as we drove along he'd been thinking how, in fact, nothing was the same.

"I'll pull myself together," he said abruptly, turning away from me to mop at his eyes. "I'm sorry, Chule."

"That's okay, Dad. Please don't feel bad," I said lamely, struggling for the right words. Inside I fumed. Why couldn't my parents have their meltdowns in private? What the hell was a kid supposed to do? I begrudgingly touched my father's hand. He soon pulled away, embarrassed. Then he turned the engine back on and took me to Palaia's for my pants. By the time we headed home he'd cheered up, goofing around to make me forget the whole episode. I didn't, of course. I was beginning to see my dad in a whole new light, as broken somehow, maybe even unfixable.

Blanche and Jerry Collins

When this will reach you I don't know, but when it does you will understand when it was written and why. Today is Good Friday and a large crowd of Catholic Marines attended the services. I imagine our thoughts were similar. I thought of all of you back home preparing for Easter. Mother getting her Easter Mass [music] polished, Sis getting her Easter clothes, and Dad as always standing by ready to drive out on some errand. All the countless memories I have of home are wonderful. I don't believe many have had as good a life as I have. Now, no matter what may come up or what I may be called on to do I'll never be afraid. My past life has been the best and if I have a future it will be even better. I am sure I'll be seeing all of you again so don't worry. There are certain to be lapses with no news but keep watching the mailbox.

All my love, Jerry

(March 30, 1945)

Aboard the troopship *George C. Clymer*, two days away from Okinawa, Private First Class Jerry Collins scribbled a brief, censored "V-Mail" to his family in Branford while his fellow Marines dashed off similar brave-faced letters home. Crammed into fetid, sardine-can quarters, the Leathernecks apprehensively awaited the first sighting of their destination: the island of Okinawa, the largest of the Ryukyu chain located only 350 nautical miles from Kyūshū, Japan. Okinawa was to be the last stepping-stone before US forces attacked Japan's home islands. The coming invasion, code named Operation Iceberg, was intended to wrest control of Okinawa from Japanese occupying forces and turn it into a staging ground for the endgame already dubbed Operation Doomsday.

The months of planning and training on Guadalcanal had culminated in the launch of the greatest armada assembled in naval history, larger even than D-Day landing forces at Normandy. Committed to the operation were 1,457 ships, 430 troopships, 300 B-29 bombers plus another 1,500 or so planes, and an initial assault force of over 180,000 men; half a million ultimately would be involved. Part of the Third Amphibious Corps under the command of Major General Roy Geiger, Jerry Collins's division the "Striking Sixth" alone accounted for 24,000 men.

The armada churning toward Okinawa occupied thirty square miles of Pacific Ocean, filling its passengers with awe and surging confidence. At the same time they all were aware that Japan's relentless ferocity in combat required the most lethal offense possible, a lesson American leaders had been slow to learn. The gruesome details of the Bataan Death March of 1942 were long kept quiet but by now every enlisted man knew how the enemy sometimes treated its prisoners. Furthermore, the Japanese forces on Okinawa were expecting the Americans. While Jerry's unit was boondocking through the jungles of the Canal, Japan's Thirty-second Army on Okinawa had been rapidly arming and fortifying under the leadership of Lieutenant General Mitsuru Ushijima and his chief of staff Major General Isamu Cho, with brilliant tactical assistance from Colonel Hiromichi Yahara. Every man on board knew that a shocking mortality rate was predicted on the beaches of Okinawa—far higher than Iwo Jima.

Another element would make the fight for Okinawa especially grisly. US propaganda had hardened the fighting men with depictions of subhuman, yellow-skinned, vicious, and diabolical "Japs," a.k.a. "Nips," creating in their minds an enemy deserving of destruction. But another group waited on Okinawa besides the reviled Japanese. For the first time, Americans in the Pacific would engage the enemy on ground inhabited by a large noncombatant population.

Japan had annexed Okinawa in 1879, eventually incorporating it as one of forty-nine prefectures. The Okinawans—"Okies" to the Americans—were ethnically and linguistically distinct from the Japanese, who considered them inferior. At the time of Operation Iceberg more than half a million Okinawans lived on the island. Many would be impressed by the Japanese into hard labor and military service. A few would throw their lot in with the Americans. All would be caught between two relentless, hammering forces. Of this Jerry and his cohorts had no idea. And even if they had, they could never have imagined the consequences.

While training on Guadalcanal, enlisted men like Jerry Collins had been kept in the dark about their coming operation. Rumors flew "thick as the mosquitoes," as he put it, but nothing was known—except that the battle would be of a massive scale. In preparation, the intelligence section had honed its scouting and patrolling skills throughout the torrential downpours of early 1945. Drenched and beat they returned to camp ready to unwind with beer and Coke rations, food packages from home, and conversation. "It seems that we all wake up here at lights out. Right after taps is the time when all the bull sessions begin with more different arguments than you have ever heard in your life," Jerry wrote home. "Our tongues seem to require more exercise than the rest of our bodies."

February 25, 1945, was the hottest day he'd ever known, and he spent as much of it as he could lying in his hammock, writing letters. "The Pacific Theater is really humming these days but there is still a long way to go. There is so much involved besides the actual fighting in an operation. Most people at home figure the war by newspaper accounts and maps alone, and fail to realize how much work is entailed in making preparations, getting supplies, and reorganizing. . . . I have no idea as to when we'll be committed to action but the more I see of this outfit in its training the more confident I feel we can't be anything but successful. We are certainly highly trained in our specific jobs."

On March 19, in his last letter before shipping out, Jerry wrote, "The Marines at Iwo Jima suffered heavy losses [the battle on Iwo had just ended] but continued to go on in their glorious manner by exacting a severe kill of Japs. The battering ram is coming into play and the question is how long the door [will] hold up. Sooner or later this outfit will have a shoulder against that weakening door."

On April 1, 1945, that day arrived. The Marine landing on Okinawa was known as L-Day, or "Love Day," to distinguish it from D-Day. As it happened, Love Day fell on Easter Sunday. It was April Fool's Day, too.

The Striking Sixth had rehearsed amphibious landings on Guadalcanal—the relentless Marine-style slog from the boats through the waves and across the sand to secure the beachhead under heavy fire. Now it was time for Jerry to experience the real thing. In the grey hours before dawn he awoke to the deafening roar of naval gunfire bombarding the landing sites to clear the way. Around 3 AM he joined the chow line, forcing down the traditional battle-day breakfast of steak and eggs. Then, checking his gear, strapping on his pack, he clambered into his assigned landing craft, which took its place in the eight-mile-long chain chugging toward the lightening shore.

Praise the Lord
And swing into position,
Can't afford to be a politician.
Praise the Lord,
We're all between perdition
And the deep blue sea!

Praise the Lord
We're on a mighty mission!

All aboard! We ain't a-goin' fishin'.
Praise the Lord,
And pass the ammunition,
And we'll all stay free!

(1943 World War II fighting man's song)

*   *   *

As I finished second grade my family's Time of Troubles was coming to a head. It felt as if a hammer hung above us, waiting to strike.

My parent's disputes were turning openly ugly and increasingly physical. Still floundering after the loss of his one good job, selling hospital equipment, Dad had grown sullen and secretive, erupting unpredictably. He broke my mother's nose during one brawl, while she turned to pots and pans and plates for weapons. Usually the blows were exchanged when we kids weren't in the room, but I was caught in the cross fire more than once. One time I was drenched with the bowl of water Mom had aimed at Dad's face, and another time I wound up with a bruise on my forehead when I darted between the two of them, throwing my arms around my mother.

The fighting sometimes brought the Branford police to 101 PO, I remember the flashing lights pulling into our driveway, the sharp knock on the door, the foot-shuffling embarrassment of the two cops when they saw our panicked faces. Their uniforms scared me but the inept talking-tos they gave Mom and Dad were infinitely worse, proof that nobody could help us.

By now I'd begun to side with Mom because she was clearly the worse off. After all, in her case there was no paramour, whereas Dad's flirtations were not limited to Mrs. Ketchum. There also was a brief fling with the mother of another of my pals. And Mom, in one of her inebriated woebegone monologues, had hinted at the existence of a third "floozy."

Dad also had the advantage over Mom when it came to booze. He handled it better physically and recovered faster. He did a lot of his drinking on the road, coming home at night stinking of liquor. One Saturday afternoon he was already tanked when he drove Mom and my sister and me to the grocery store. The car weaved from side to side while my mother sobbed that he was sure to kill us all. Trapped in the backseat I listened to them disputing who had the real drinking problem and who was simply reacting to the other's bad behavior. I grabbed the door handle thinking, "open it, open it, open it," imagining myself spilling onto the road. With the screech of brakes, Mom and Dad would race toward my bleeding body, reunited in guilty remorse. It infuriated me that I didn't have the nerve to try it. I pressed the button and felt the door release, but that was as far as I went. Not long after that excursion, the cops hauled Dad in for drunken driving and eventually he lost his license for a while, a potential death knell for a salesman. He drove anyway. He even had a fender bender right in front of Branford High School. He rammed into the Driver's Ed car during the middle of the school day while a DMV rep was on the scene administering road tests to BHS students. That sent a tidal wave of gossip rushing through the high school hallways that caught up with one of my brothers, appalling and humiliating him.

While Dad could pretend to function, alcohol hit Mom like a sledgehammer. It robbed her of her natural grace and gnawed away at her beauty. In those days a drunk dad was a bad thing but a drunk mom was a crime against nature. In her humiliation my mother became a stealth addict, hiding her bottles throughout the house and yard. I found sticky glasses hidden in a corner of the old garage, squeezed between the protruding roots of a tree trunk, tucked into one of the tin cans my brother Chip had embedded in the lawn so he could practice his putting. I brought my finds into the house and left them in the sink, hoping, I guess, to shame

Mom so she'd stop. The glasses simply got washed and returned to the cupboard.

That June my oldest brother graduated first in his high school class. Early on commencement day Mom closeted herself with a bottle. As the evening hour approached when Chip would deliver the valedictory address, she resurfaced, totally smashed but determined to attend. When Dad told her she would have to stay home, she erupted in incoherent rage, weeping and flailing about. Finally he strong-armed her into the cellar, the only room in the house that had a lock on the door. Otherwise she would have staggered all the way to the high school and disrupted the proceedings. Even when drunk, Mom's force of will was unconquerable.

In my memory my sister and I were left at home to block Mom's escape by sitting outside on the rusty cellar bulkhead, which had no lock. I heard her crying on the other side as she banged on the metal, begging for us to release her. I yearned to comply, but I was terrified she'd attack us if she got out, like a rabid raccoon let out of a cage. It seems impossible that Miff and I really were left alone to act as jailers, but that's what I remember. Later I heard about my brother's great speech. My mother never got over missing her boy's big day, although she managed to forget why she wasn't there, preferring to believe she was the victim of wanton cruelty.

With any skirmish there is a weirdly peaceful aftermath, when the battered combatants reel off to heal for the next round. After that wretched night my mother revived and continued to cook for all of us, numbly performing her other household routines. Every morning my father downed his black coffee and drove away, presumably on his insurance sales route. My grandmother, meanwhile, cruised off in her Ford to play bridge or visit friends, attend her book group or garden club or choir rehearsal, maintaining her high spirits through a busy social life that kept her son and his family at arm's length.

At last school let out. In the merciful summer warmth our home took on a different personality. The doors were open and the windows let in the hopeful sounds of a larger world. All of us, including the many cats and Handsome Dan, Angy's adopted dachshund, escaped the confines of 101 PO as much as possible. The boys had summer jobs at the Pine Orchard Club, Peter washing dishes in the kitchen, Patrick working for "Farmer" John Skillman the tennis pro, and Chip as king of the caddies under golf pro Stan "Prune" Starzec. And Jennifer was making her own pals now, so she and I weren't attached at the hip anymore. At the end of the day we all came together for dinner. "Bless us this house each brick and rafter, may it be filled with peace and laughter," read the old trivet on which Mom set the hot plates. After dish drying I ran over to Collins Drive, for games or hanging-out that went on till sunset. When darkness finally settled in, I came home and sat on the back stoop for a while, watching the fireflies. That year millions of them sparkled across our lawn, in earthly competition with the stars.

I began to spend all my free time with my best friend Stacey Ketchum. She was a Mexican jumping bean kind of kid, not a moody ponderer like me. Her feistiness and smart mouth appealed to me. Sometimes she was mean but she was also capable of impetuously generous acts and an easy affection I badly needed. I was shy, pasty, and plump at that age, from spending too much time alone reading, with a blunt haircut that didn't suit me. Stacey, in contrast, was super mod in her boldly patterned micro-mini shifts and bell-bottoms. Skinny, with matchstick limbs, she had stringy, dirty blonde hair a la Twiggy and enormous eyes of an eerily unclassifiable color, a sort of brownish silvery smoke.

Stacey liked to hang out at my house. She regularly slept over on *Creature Feature* night, when we stayed up late pinching and poking to spook each other. My mother grew agitated over the constant presence of Mrs. Ketchum's daughter, however, and by midsummer she put a stop to these overnights. In one of her sodden states she also punished me for the first time, forbidding me to play with Stacey for a week. Once she sobered up I could tell she'd forgotten what she'd done, and I ignored the prohibition and went over to Stacey's instead.

Hers was one of the stunted, hastily built houses on Collins Drive with the least attention to architectural niceties. Painted a sour mustard color, it seemed barely finished inside, the undersized rooms furnished with cheap contemporary designs. I liked the vinyl-upholstered breakfast nook, though, which looked just like the ones I'd seen in kitchens on TV. The careless casualness of the house, the general aura of disdain for homemaking, suited Mrs. Ketchum very well. She was definitely not a homebody. I rarely encountered Stacey's dad, a pinched, downtrodden-looking man with sad eyes and straw-colored hair who was gone most of the time, working I guess, to support the three children he'd begun acquiring at a young age.

To be fair, Mrs. Ketchum was invariably kind and friendly to me. She always had treats for us: instant pudding or Jell-O, KoolPops, gingerbread made from a Jiffy mix and topped with CoolWhip. I associated her with all things modern and easy and offhanded. Occasionally she took us on outings, a novelty for me because Mom couldn't drive and my road-weary father never wanted to go far on the weekends. It was always a thrill when Mrs. Ketchum put on her fashionable bug-eyed shades and we climbed into her late-model car to head somewhere frivolous, on the spur of the moment. Sometimes she took us and some other Collins Drive kids to a big beach up the coast in Madison that made Branford Point look puny. Or we might dash off on a shopping spree in New Haven, where on one occasion Stacey scored a pair of white go-go boots. She and her mom were at home wandering through department store displays in the big city, whereas I felt like a country bumpkin with my window-shopping eyes and empty purse.

I picked up occasional hints that Dad was a presence in Stacey's house. She mentioned my dad and her mom were friends, and he'd been over when her daddy was out. Mrs. Ketchum told me flat out that she thought my father was very good looking. Eventually she went further, confiding when I was alone with her that she and Dad were thinking about divorcing to marry each other and raise all of us kids together. "Would you like that? Wouldn't that be nice?" I was flabbergasted, frightened, but even more, I was confused. I was too young to fathom what these misbehaving adults were up to. Would this mean Mom would be sent away and Mrs. Ketchum would take her place? I imagined her dressed in a bridal gown, standing next to my dad. Making our dinner. Tucking me in at night. But instead of protesting or running off to tell my mommy, I acted as if I hadn't heard. "I have to go home for dinner now," I bleated, scooting out the door. After that I was more on edge whenever my parents argued. Should I tell on Dad and Mrs. Ketchum? If I did would that only make the threat come true and tear up my family? My secret became a grenade I could toss at any moment. I clutched it tightly.

One afternoon Dad took Miff and me to Branford Point, something we no longer did as a family. In fact, my mother had stopped going altogether. I saw Mrs. Ketchum before they did. She was lying on a blanket in her bikini. Mrs. Ketchum had a poster-girl allure that made my ailing mother look doubly haggard and worn. Her two youngest children were playing in the water, her husband probably working. Watching my father intently, I saw his expression change the instant he spotted her. I went hot inside. This meeting was planned. They would keep their distance in public, pretending to attend to their children while ogling each other across a discreet divide. Failing in his latest sales job, his stock tumbling in our family, Dad was trying to prove himself in a grotesque new way. He used Miff and me as pawns to escape from the combat zone back home. I spent many days at the beach that summer, watching the signals pass between Dad and Mrs. Ketchum. Eventually I became inured to the adult games, preferring my own amusements.

By August, however, Dad had grown reckless. He barely concealed his visits to our neighbor's house on nights when Mr. Ketchum must have been working a late shift. Once I couldn't sleep and went downstairs, where I found Mom standing in the kitchen in the dark, with a drink in her hand, staring off toward our neighbor's house. "Look, honey," she said in a strange, weary voice. "Stacey's mommy left a light on to signal your daddy." I obediently went to her side and saw where she was pointing. The night was quiet, the beam of one small bulb steady and hot. I began to cry, careful not to make a sound.

✳   ✳   ✳

Dear Folks,

I am writing this while on the way to combat. . . . Please don't worry because I know how to take care of myself and you'll be hearing from me after it is over. . . . Our last base was Guadalcanal in case you couldn't figure it out and we are now approaching our target on the sea. I haven't seen a sign of fear among the men and you can be sure this will bring typical Marine Corps results. Love to you all, Jerry.

(Love Day, Easter Sunday, 1945)

As his amtrac—amphibious tractor—trundled through sloshing waves toward the northern end of Okinawa's Hagushi beaches, Jerry Collins waited in tense excitement for his first glimpse of the enemy. The second the Marines set foot on sand they would begin their interminable, hair-raising dash through a torrent of hot metal spewing from machine gun nests and heavy artillery.

The amtrac touched bottom, its operator lowered the ramp, and the men, nerves on fire, stomachs and bowels uneasy, clambered into the water: Advance—advance—advance! Now Jerry would witness Marine brethren lurching and dropping all around him in the random selection of the day's first casualties. His duty was to keep going, no matter what.

Instead of a firestorm, though, an eerie stillness greeted the charging Marines. The men gazed about them, mystified. Light-headed with surprise and relief, Jerry loped over the sand. Soon the beach was littered with unused gas masks as the Leathernecks lightened their loads.

The four divisions landing that day were virtually unopposed. For the rest of his life Dad marveled at the surreal quiet that greeted the Marines on Love Day. Other than pockets of resistance, some fitful mortar and sniper fire, their enemy was nowhere in sight. A week of bombarding, the heaviest ever to support a naval landing, had preceded the American fleet's arrival, to "soften up" the enemy forces before the men debarked and headed for shore. Had all that bombing done the trick? Were the Japanese already defeated?

In fact, the bombardment was ineffectual, a monumental waste; the enemy waited at the other end of the island, underground. In response to a string of crushing defeats, the Japanese had switched fighting tactics. Rather than launch doomed banzai charges against superior American firepower, they were digging in to fight as long as possible, to the last man. This new approach, defense-in-depth, which showed up on Peleliu and Iwo Jima, was far more elaborate and well executed on Okinawa. Ushijima's Thirty-second Army had spent months building elaborate networks of fortified underground tunnels and caves, to which the Japanese soldiers withdrew during bombing raids. Afterward, they could move in close to the invading forces, leaping from cave openings and shallow "spider holes" to lob grenades or tear into startled Americans with machine guns zeroed in to inflict the worst damage possible.

On Love Day, euphoria swept over Jerry's division: Hey, this war is nearly over! The Japanese know they're whipped! However, a bitter surprise was in store for the overconfident Marines. Okinawa would prove to be the Pacific war's most savage and costly island campaign. It would last eighty-two days and leave more than a quarter of a million people dead.

CHAPTER SIX DAD'S
THEME SONG

Blanche Collins with her daughter Julia

Grab your coat and get your hat,
Leave your worries on the doorstep,
Just direct your feet
To the sunny side of the street.
Can't you hear a pitterpat?
And that happy tune is your step,
Life can be so sweet,
On the sunny side of the street.

("On the Sunny Side of the Street")

Thanks to Dad and Angy, who had great pipes, and Mom who didn't but adored music, I was humming and singing as soon as I could carry a tune, one note chasing another through my brain all day long. When my sister caught up we made a duo. Starting at two and four years old we'd prance into the living room damp and shiny after our shared bath to put on impromptu song-and-dance routines for Angy. "You naughty girls," she gasped, pretending to be shocked, a shapely hand pressed to her bosom quaking with mirth. "Cavorting about in your birthday suits!" Dad watched from the sidelines, chortling and egging us on till Mom finally came after us with towels, afraid we'd catch cold or else wear out our welcome with our imperious grandma.

This trio of grownups shaped my musical sensibility. The family diva, Angy's tastes ranged from highfalutin opera to witty Gilbert and Sullivan, from eclectic folk songs, Tin Pan Alley tunes, and vaudevillian numbers to Negro spirituals. Morning at 101 PO often began with a boisterous duet as my grandmother attacked the old Acrosonic accompanied by howling Handsome Dan, our dachshund. Mom preferred classical and choral music and show tunes. Our devoted fan, she was always putting in for some request—"You Are My Sunshine," "Favorite Things," or one of the sentimental ditties she favored.

Dad's influence far surpassed theirs, however, because his feeling for his music was unmistakably profound and complicated and mysterious, even to me as a child. While he liked a few contemporary singers, his phonograph needle was forever circling the groove of the thirties and forties. His attachment to that era went soul deep; you could see it in his face whenever a jazz age maestro spun on the turntable.

I remember his kidlike glee when he brought home a fancy Magnavox cabinet stereo system, paid for on credit, and showed me how to operate it with tender fingers. He promptly joined a record club and soon Tommy Dorsey, Count Basie, Clancy Hayes, Duke Ellington, Louis "Satchmo" Armstrong, and Benny Goodman were arriving in the mail, along with Mantovani, Mozart, Chopin, the Mormon Tabernacle Choir, Broadway albums and the like, to please Mom. "Jerry, we can't afford this," she yelped, dismayed, when one batch arrived. He promised to return the records right away so we wouldn't be billed. Of course he never did, so eventually Mom took matters into her own hands and canceled the account. But by then Dad had already acquired a thick stack of albums. "Look what's come in the mail, girls," he said, whenever the flat cardboard carton arrived. "Wait'll you see what I picked out for us this month."

He eagerly taught his favorites to his daughters, his mellow baritone anchoring our flitty sparrow sopranos. His wartime standards formed the core of my repertoire, from the peppy "Don't Sit Under the Apple Tree" to the swingy storytelling of "Beale Street Blues" to the melancholy "I'll Be Seeing You," with which he serenaded my mother during their courting days. He liked songs with attitude and style, especially the Andrews Sisters' ebullient hits like "Hold Tight" and Cab Calloway's famous scatting. He assumed his cool-cat posture as he biddly-oh-ho-hayed and skiddle-iddle-dee-at-do-dayed to his daughters' delight, regaling us with musical tales of the boogie-woogie washerwoman of Harlem and the Texas honky-tonk piano man. From his old seabag he also hauled out the Marine Hymn—teaching us ALL the verses—along with some smartass ditties that had circulated among the homesick WWII fighting men, like:

> Goodbye, Mama, I'm off to Yokohama for the red, white, and blue, my country and you!
> Goodbye, Mama, I'm off to Yokohama just to teach all those Japs the Yanks are no saps. A million fighting sons of Uncle Sam, if you please, will soon have all those Japs right down on their Japa-knees!
> So goodbye, Mama, I'm off to Yokohama for my country, my flag and you!

("We sang that two ways, switching Okinawa for Yokohama," my dad explained.)

Another cynical little number went something like:

> Through the dust clouds yearning
> Keep the home fires burning
> While the boys are far away
> They're whooping it up back home!

But of all the melodies dating from his war, one occupied a special niche as Dad's theme song. He always sang "On the Sunny Side of the Street" with special verve and feeling. "Sunny Side" seemed to pep him up when his mood turned melancholy. Sometimes he even rendered it à la Satchmo, right down to the throaty "Oh, YEAAAHHHHHHHHH" at the end, his arms flung wide, a ludicrous grin on his face.

I grew tired of that song, and the Satchmo schtick first became annoying, then embarrassing, as I aged from little kid to big. One time I peevishly asked my dad why he sang "Sunny Side" so much. I could tell that hurt his feelings. He thought for a minute before answering. Then he told me how the Marines on Okinawa slept out in the open in foxholes or, sometimes, inside the ancestral tombs dotting the island. One time, during a lull in the fighting, he and his buddies had lucked into better shelter: a hut abandoned by an Okinawan family that had probably gone off to hide in the caves. Inside the hut the Marines found a Japanese Victrola and American phonograph records. They stole some time from the war to sit around listening to jazz, echoes from home. It was Louis Armstrong belting out "Sunny Side" that had stayed stuck in Dad's mind throughout the ugly days that followed. "Like a lucky charm," he said. That song got stuck in my mind too as my father tried to fend off the creeping blues and hang onto the positive attitude that was slipping away, his wife and family along with it.

* * *

Dear Mom,

How are you? I am fine. When will you come home? I miss you. Yesterday M [an older friend] came and took us to Grandel's Pond. Mrs. Grandel [a neighbor] took Miff next door to the Dumkoskis and got Miff some BOY skates. She is good at them. M gave me a pair. I can do it a little. M ate over (dinner). In February we are going to see DOCTOR DOOLITTLE!

Come home, Love, Julie

P.S. I want you to come home.

P.S.S. I love you.

P.S.S.S. Write back.

P.S.S.S.S. Please!

P.S.S.S.S.S. Sweets to the Sweet.

P.S.S.S.S.S.S. Hope you like candy. [enclosed]

P.S.S.S.S.S.S.S. I love you.

(January 28, 1968, to Mrs. Blanche G. Collins at Connecticut Valley Hospital)

In the fall of 1967 I blubbered goodbye as my oldest brother left for Harvard. Chip's departure foretold an avalanche of loss. Before long I knew that Patrick would go away too, and then Peter. There had been safety in our numbers; we five kids had given each other cover and softened our parents' impact. I was scared of a future without the boys around, but my own third-grader fixation on making friends and fitting in soon distracted me.

With Mom slurring and sleepy by dusk it fell to Dad to tuck his girls in and hear our prayers every night. He lulled us with the weakening magic of his promises—of a better job, parental harmony, nice new clothes and fat weekly allowances, and marvelous trips we would all take together. I noticed, though, that he kept circling back to his life as a hard-charging Marine, when his purpose and place were clear, his family a band of true-blue buddies who didn't make demands. Sometimes I wanted to holler: Shut up about that war, those men! I'm a little girl! You're my daddy! Stop being friends with Mrs. Ketchum! Stop letting Mom drink! Go out and make some money like you keep promising!

I can't remember anything about my mother from that fall. She disappears until an afternoon in early winter when I came home from school and couldn't find her. Often she was holed up in the master bedroom, pretending to nap, but that day it was empty. In fact, nobody was home at all. The house was cold and spooky with late-afternoon shadows waving on the walls, filling me with anxiety. I went out without my coat to see if Mom was bringing in the laundry, which she hung on the clothesline even in winter, to save on electricity. A thaw had set in and the snow-crusted earth was melting into a sad state of grey slush. I sloshed through the back yard calling Ma, Ma, Ma, until I spotted a dark blotch against the snow at the edge of the woods. I approached slowly, my heart ramming into my chest. That blotch was my mother, spread-eagled on the ground near the Indian Prayer Rock, her face grey in the unkind light. An empty bottle lay a few inches from her open hand. I dropped to my knees beside her and began to screech.

Did somebody answer my screams? Did I run to a neighbor's house? Did I clutch my mother whimpering until another family member arrived? I have no idea. After that afternoon Mom was missing. That's all I remember.

My sister and I were fed some hooey that she was overworked and went away to get rest, to a hospital across the state. Nothing was said about that bottle. At first I felt huge relief. Life was peaceful all of a sudden. No more brawling parents. No more glass clinking in the night. No moaning sobs or clenched angry voices. Some grownups were helping Mom. She would come home soon, restored to her old ebullient self, and she and Dad would love each other again.

It didn't take long, however, before the silence grew upsetting. Weeks went by with no contact. Apparently Mom was too exhausted to pay any attention yet to the family she'd left behind. Valentine's Day passed, and although Miff and I came home from school with fat bundles of valentines from our classmates, we didn't receive any from Mom—a shocking omission. St. Patrick's Day, her birthday, came and went too, but we hadn't the heart to put on the green and white ribbons and the *Erin go bragh* pins our Polish mother had stored away for that occasion. Then all at once it was Easter Sunday, and we awoke to find Easter baskets waiting by our beds.

The sight of them put a pout on my face. These weren't our real baskets—our pretty berry-picking baskets that Mom loaded up year after year with candy and trinkets, fastening flowers and ribbon and pipe-cleaner birds with feathered tails to the handles. "A dentist's delight," my father had called Mom's pagan offerings. No, the cellophane-covered baskets waiting for us that Mom-less morning were the impersonal creations of some supermarket. Dad had done his best, but in the role of Peter Cottontail he was a lousy stand-in for our mom.

Far more than her special basket I missed my mother the harbinger of spring. Every Easter she greedily sniffed the warming air, pointing out the hopeful signs of a world starting over: how the days were getting noticeably longer, the forsythia was out, the first robin had sung, the trees were all in bud. Mom savored the subtle changes nobody else bothered about and without her I went partially blind.

That day shattered my kid's complacency. With the help of gossipy neighborhood kids I'd already begun to piece together the truth—that the Connecticut Valley Hospital was a jail of sorts, place of last resort for loonies and addicts and other lost souls. Sneering jokesters dubbed it "Happy Valley." And I was sick deep inside with the certainty that I'd helped drive my mother there. I hadn't tried hard enough to be good, to make her happy. Worse still, my best friend was the daughter of Mrs. Ketchum, who I'd picked over my darling mother by running to the enemy camp every chance I got. Perhaps if I'd ratted on Mrs. Ketchum and Dad things would have turned out differently.

Now she was in a mental ward. No one would say for how long. So for the first time ever, Miff and I didn't dress up in our usual Easter finery and my family skipped the mass, although my grandmother went, performing her organist duties as usual. My father vanished for a good part of the day, maybe drinking, maybe driving off some remorse. I wondered if he was with Mrs. Ketchum but decided no, she'd stick with her family on a holiday. Besides, he didn't seem to be meeting her lately, at least not that I knew, and she'd become cooler toward me when I was over.

Come evening I skipped dinner and lay on my bed, worn out from sadness. After the sound of dishwashing had stopped my father came in quietly. "Chule?" He sat next to me. "Are you okay?"

I nodded into the pillow. "What's up, kiddo? Bad case of phooz-ma?" *Phoozma* was a versatile word he'd made up to diagnose the blues that afflicted most everybody at one time or another. One time he'd let me skip school, earnestly explaining in his note that I suffered from phoozma that day.

I shook my head, my throat too knotted to release any words. He sighed heavily, his hand warming the middle of my spine, and then for the first time since Mom left he tried to tell the truth. "I screwed up, Julie, but I'm going to work hard to get Mom to forgive me. Lately I haven't been a good husband or father. I'll do better, I promise. But you have to realize, honey, your mother has a bad drinking problem. She's in the hospital because she wants to get better."

I thought about this. "You drink too, Dad," I whispered.

"Yeah, but I can stop. I will stop. Your mother can't. Not without medical help."

It took all my nerve to ask him: "You love Mom, right, Daddy? As much as ever?" I saw it again—that imaginary wedding portrait of him and Mrs. Ketchum.

"Of course I do," he said loudly, instantly on the defensive. "But for the life of me, Chule, nothing satisfies your mother. And I'm doing the best I can."

"You are not!" I retorted, stung by his retreat from accountability. "You just said—" His hand turned to lead on my back, each finger digging in. Then he stood up so fast the loose springs did a noisy jig. "I can't take this." His voice was choked. "I can't take any more, goddammit. I don't know which way to turn to please you people." He fled from the room, from me, all at once his little enemy.

Moments later I heard him pacing up and down the gravel driveway. I longed to yell out my window and plead with him to come back, but I was terrified that he would ignore me, his pain-in-the-ass daughter.

By May Miff and I finally began to receive regular letters from Mom. She tried her best to sound chipper while ignoring the question of when she would come home. Occasionally my father, but usually one or more of my brothers, drove us to see her in Middletown, an hour away. En route we always stopped at a pharmacy to buy Jean Naté cologne, scented soaps, or a Whitman Sampler. My sister and I only visited on nice days, when we could meet her at the picnic tables outdoors because she never wanted us to glimpse the inside of her new home. I wouldn't have noticed the ugly setting anyway, because my attention was locked onto Mom. Her hair had grown long, silvering in places. She looked older from hard living, and younger with the booze out of her system. Her green eyes were clear and bright again. She hardly smiled, though, and her attention strayed a lot. I wondered if our visits were more pain than pleasure for her. Sometimes she brought a friend along, an older woman named Lily, who served as a gentle buffer.

The few times he took us to Connecticut Valley Dad tried to charm Mom. She kept him at a distance. As he juggled single parenthood and his sales rounds he grew more careworn and subdued, but also, at times, downright cantankerous, obviously uncomfortable in his new domestic role. Angy helped with cooking and occasionally took Miff and me along on her social rounds. Mostly, though, Dad was in charge. That meant a lot of burnt barbecue and dinner from some cans, erratic bedtimes, unwashed and unmended clothing, neglected hygiene, a grubby house. His sense of humor disappeared and there was no more singing, no bedtime games. He began having us tuck ourselves in at night, with the half-hearted instruction, "Don't forget to say your prayers, girls." He was more nervous and skittish than usual—one day the explosive sound of a backfiring car sent him to the ground hollering, "Hit the deck!" But on the plus side, he was too burdened by present cares to dwell much on that old war of his, and he drank less.

Occasionally he roused himself and attempted to jolly my sister and me into better moods. During a particularly dark patch he introduced the Zorro game, which involved sneaking into our room at night and inking a lightning-bolt Z either on my forehead or Miff's. At breakfast the following morning his jaw would drop as he pointed to one of us with bug-eyed astonishment. "Good Lord, girls! It's—the—Mark—of—ZORRO!" The victim always ran giggling to the mirror to look.

One day Dad made a surprising announcement. He was taking us girls on one of his sales trips. In early January my sister and I had gone along when he drove Chip to St. John's College in Annapolis, Maryland, where my brother transferred because he hadn't liked Harvard. I guess Dad thought another road trip might do his mopey daughters some good.

On a late spring afternoon we set out with Dad in the station wagon. The plan was to stay at a motel that night, and Miff and I would accompany him on his sales calls the next morning. Whoopee—that meant skipping a whole day of school! "We'll have a ball," my father promised. "And you'll see your Daddy in action." He launched into an upbeat explanation of how he prepared to meet with clients by doing some research and making strategic calls, filling out file cards he studied beforehand, determining the key points to stress with each person to clinch the sale. Personality was key, he said. Knowing how to connect with people. The nature of my father's work was a mystery, other than the fact that it was unreliable and took him on the road a lot. I wasn't all that interested in learning more, but having him pay so much concentrated attention to us was a novelty, and I loved any excuse to get in the car and go someplace.

To this day I'm not sure where we wound up that night, but when I drive along the stretch of Route 95 right below New York City, the industrial, dehumanized landscape conjures that long-ago fieldtrip. It was dark when we left the highway and drove into the parking lot of a Howard Johnson's Motor Lodge—a far cry, Dad said, from the ritzy Commander in New Orleans or other fancy-pants hotels where he used to stay when he had that fabulous job selling hospital equipment. Miff and I were delighted regardless. I was thrilled with the calm, orderly setting, the solicitous behavior of the desk clerk, my father's masterful poise. I loved our room with its big bland furnishings, beige carpeting, and antiseptic spotless-ness—no wincing floorboards, no dust bunnies under the bed, no cracked windowpanes letting in talons of cold, no spiders dangling in the corners.

We ate dinner at the motel restaurant. This was deluxe, all right! Laminated menus, sparkly formica tabletops, leatherette seats, and uniformed waitresses rushing about with their pads and coffeepots. "Order anything you want on the menu, girls. We'll get some dessert too," said our daddy, the man of the world.

Afterward Miff and I watched TV in our room while he went to "make some phone calls." I'd begun to fret by the time the key rattled and he strolled in, wafting a familiar eighty-proof perfume. The smell jolted me like a cattle prod. He'd said he was going to stop! Maybe he saw my anxiety because he quickly turned into Mr. Jolly, entertaining us with stories and songs—including "Sunny Side," which he performed standing up, as usual, striding back and forth, hamming it up. After that he revived the old "bouncy-wouncy-woo" game, jouncing us up and down on the springy motel mattress, which caused Miff to shriek with delight but left me irri-table. I went to sleep with a headache, inching as far away as I could from my pungent father, who lay between us like a stiff on a gurney.

In the morning we girls savored our HoJo pancakes, using up all the foil butter pats and the little plastic syrups and asking for more. Dad sipped his black coffee in silence. Then he said, abruptly, "A change in plans, girls." He'd decided we shouldn't tag along after all. He had to keep up a fast pace. We'd be bored, cooling our heels in assorted lobbies. He would buy us comics and puzzle books and we could watch TV in the room until he came to get us at checkout time.

When he returned a few hours later he quickly packed up the single suitcase and hustled us into the car. Something was wrong. There was no boasting about a big sale. No amusing anecdotes about clients he'd successfully "bamboozled" or "hoodwinked"— Dad liked that swindler sort of talk. Long after our trip I would wonder if he actually made a single sales call that day. Was it all a pretense? Had he lost his nerve? After he left us in the HoJo room, did he drive around the strange streets aimlessly, killing time?

An hour later the station wagon broke down on the highway, in a despairingly final fashion. My father flipped out, cursing and banging on the wheel while my sister and I cowered. When he collected himself he got out of the car, slamming the door. In a seedy trench coat he stood in the unseasonably icy drizzle, struggling to raise the hood, fiddling beneath ineffectually. He knew nothing about cars, his lack of manly handiness long having been a point of contention between him and Mom. Hmmmmmph, I judged, turning snottier by the second. Now his ineptitude meant we were stuck in the middle of nowhere. Finally a cop pulled over and called in to get a tow truck for us. Unfortunate news: because of the weather many motorists were in trouble and it would be a while before help came. Trapped in the car Miff and I played McHale's Navy, which involved locating the fattest raindrop on the window, and the license plate game. We also sang songs, my father joining in, attempting to be a good sport. "NO, NO, NO, NOT THAT ONE," I cried, covering my ears when Dad inevitably launched into his theme song. He shut up immediately, while I sizzled with the pleasing power of brattiness. "The Ants Go Marching," I suggested to Miff, who enthusiastically chimed in on the lines she knew. But once he ran out of cigarettes Dad also ran out of patience, and at last he ordered us to sit quietly. "Girls, you're giving me a headache." After that, the hiss of tires on the slick highway and the foggy faces in passing automobiles were our entertainment.

We'd been stuck for several hours by the time I saw the flashing light approach. "There it is!" Hooray! But that tow truck raced right by us. It took another hour before my father managed to hail a second cop and finally get us our tow. At the service station the news was catastrophic—some major repair was required. Dad looked close to tears, his thin shoulders slumping in defeat. We stayed at another HoJo motel that night, which I, now a seasoned business traveler, critically compared to the first. Which décor was more pleasing? Was the restaurant as spiffy here? Wasn't this desk clerk creepy looking?

That night my father had a bad dream. His moaning woke me, and once I realized what was happening I shook him, alarmed by how cold his skin felt. He sat up like a shot, with a loud "uunngh." A moment later Miff popped up too but immediately fell back onto her pillow, deep asleep.

Dad was soaked in sweat, his worn undershirt dirty looking in the tainted light seeping in from the parking lot. "That was bad," he muttered, running a hand through his hair, leaving it on end. Then he realized I was still sitting up, shivering. He'd scared the beejezus out of me. "Hey, Chule, get back under the covers." He carefully hooked a long leg over Miff and stood up. He went over to the bureau and began patting the top, searching. I heard the match snick, saw the friendly flare as he lit a cigarette.

I lay there watching him. He came over and studied me for a moment. It's okay, go to sleep, all is well, he muttered absentmindedly. A long pause. He could tell I wasn't about to drop off, too agitated by the day's events. I never sleep through the night, he finally confided in a soft voice. It's been this way since the war.

I could have said, I know, Dad. But I didn't. I felt too cross, worried about how we'd ever get home and close to tears from missing my mother.

The next day was sunny and springlike again. Things felt much more hopeful even if they weren't. At nine Dad would telephone the service station. The guy had told him that maybe, just maybe, they could finish the work by noon. "It helped having you cuties along," Dad said brightly. "Two stranded kids—pulls at the heartstrings." He was in an upbeat, playful mood. I wondered if the sales trip had proven a success after all.

Before we went down to breakfast I wrote Mom a letter on HoJo stationery and Dad tucked in his own page. After her death I found this letter and read my late father's enclosure, in which he said he hoped she was feeling better each day and pleaded with her to get well and come home. "By now you must know that you can't take a single drink," he wrote. He promised he would straighten up his act too, because Miff and I were losing hope. "We could be happy and the children need someone to take care of them—they have a very lonely life."

Reading this short, earnest note, I recalled my dad's days of single parenthood. I decided I had underestimated how hard he tried or how much he cared. "The children come first," he wrote back then.

When Dad died Jennifer and I wanted to sing "Sunny Side" at his funeral but Mom asked us not to. She said people wouldn't understand what we meant by it. "Is that so important," I huffed, stopping short when it hit me what was really going on. Mom harbored a grudge against Dad's music because when he sneaked over to Mrs. Ketchum he always left one of his jazz records playing on the Magnavox, to make Mom think he was still in the house. It was unrealistic, cruel, even, to ask her to hear something different in Dad's theme song.

When both my parents were gone I came upon the wartime letter that mentioned the day Dad's intelligence outfit found the Victrola on which they had spun "Sunny Side," imprinting its feel-good message in his mind for the rest of his life. About a month after that I discovered that my father's Marine comrade William Manchester had recorded the same episode in his war memoir *Goodbye, Darkness,* in which Dad appeared as the shy, sharp-eyed scout "Dusty Rhodes of Yale."

Then I pictured my father performing one more time in our old playroom back at 101 PO with his arms wide open, reaching for an elusive happiness.

CHAPTER SEVEN

DAYS OF RECKONING

Jerry Collins at the rifle range

... The Nips are putting up quite a fight here at the southern end of the island. They are taking a terrific pounding from the air and from our artillery but the infantry must move slowly because they are so well entrenched. At night they shell us with their own big guns and at first it was a little frightening.... Sunday was Mother's Day and I thought of you, Mother, and of how much I would like to see you. Who knows, perhaps our next operation, whenever it comes off, will be the last. This push turned out to be a surprise. We secured two thirds of the island with no strain and are having in return our hands full with this final portion. It will all result in lots of names off Japan's pay roll.

(*May 16, 1945*)

Buoyed by the ease of Love Day, the Marines were eager to wrap up their share of the operation. In early April the Sixth Division was given the task of capturing the northern end of Okinawa. Laboring under heavy packs Jerry's regiment raced through the rugged, forested heights of the Motobu peninsula where intense skirmishing with Japanese soldiers around Mount Yae Take put an end to the notion of a cakewalk. Soon rows of American corpses awaited the body bags that had traveled with the US troops to the island.

It was the third week of April before Jerry could stop long enough to reassure his parents that all was well. "We were pretty astonished at the lack of Jap resistance," he wrote. "We had expected a tough job so near their homeland but were fooled. It wasn't all gravy, however, and some [of the Twenty-ninth Regiment] were lost or shot up and on several nights the mortar shells were coming too close for comfort. A few Japs would work in close enough to flip a grenade or two in a foxhole. At one time on an OP [observation post] I spent quite a little while pinned behind a rock by a sniper but a machine gun crew shot him down. All in all it lacked most of the horror and blood expected.... You can cease all worrying as I believe I am through as far as this operation is concerned."

After securing two-thirds of the island ahead of schedule, the Sixth Marines thought their work was done and began to unwind. The respite was brief. "Well I was wrong about being secured and once again I'm writing from a foxhole," Jerry wrote on May 11, a few miles north of the front lines in southern Okinawa. His company had headed south in early May to assist the Army—in the Marines' view, bail them out—which was paying dearly for territory held by the Japanese. "The main Nip force was at the other end of the island and we are now pushing after them. I don't know how they can take the pounding our planes and big guns are giving them but in the end the infantry will have to get them."

Enemy resistance in the south confounded the Americans. Despite the overwhelming superiority of US forces, General Ushijima's army responded with brutally effective strategic strikes. This was not the warfare of Europe: the Japanese forces fought to extinction, exactingly trained and psychologically prepared to sacrifice all lives for their Emperor. Their appalling bravery stunned the Americans, who were accustomed to foes who behaved more like themselves, and were predisposed from racism and ignorance to underestimate the Japanese.

In fact, Ushijima knew from the outset that his outnumbered troops on Okinawa had little chance of victory. The real mission was to hang in and hold out, detaining the Americans and killing as many as possible while the home islands hastily prepared for invasion. Underscoring the importance of holding Okinawa, Japan's imperial command approved an unprecedented assault it called the "Divine Wind," a succession of ten separate twilight attacks by hordes of kamikaze suicide planes targeting US destroyers, aircraft carriers, and troopships. The first "wind" gust was unleashed on April 6, the last in late June. Despite rattletrap planes and novice pilots, the kamikaze terrorized the Naval forces locked in place off-shore to support the ground campaign, ultimately killing nearly five thousand US sailors, sinking thirty-six ships, and damaging several hundred more.

Typically, US Marines like Jerry Collins served as the elite assault troops with the high-risk mission to storm in, achieve quick victory, secure the beach, and then get out, leaving the Army and other forces to mop up with their superior firepower. On Okinawa, however, the Marines soon found themselves sharing the role of battering ram. While the US ground forces pounded Ushijima's defense lines, a "typhoon of steel" from both sides blasted southern Okinawa all through April and into May. The island's green tranquillity was relentlessly transformed into a burnt and lifeless zone strewn with spent bullets and shells, charred tractors, pieces of uniforms, abandoned gear, and bodies that speedily decomposed in the hot wet climate.

As a scout-observer Jerry Collins accompanied rifle companies to the front and radioed in estimates of the numbers of enemy dead, wounded, or captured, plus information on the location and condition of enemy troops and arms in any given area in order to update the battalion situation map. Jerry also brought in lost or wounded men and examined the bodies of dead Japanese for unit identification papers. He did a lot of his work through field binoculars, but inevitably came into close contact with the enemy. On one patrol Jerry had a face-to-face encounter that he never divulged to his comrades nor wrote about to his family. It would haunt him for the rest of his years.

*　　*　　*

Dear Mom,
I am sorry I have not written much. I thought you'd be home by now. I wish you were home!!! I wish you had been at the [Parents'

Night] art exhibit. My class had two murals we made about a month ago. We had 2 or 3 folders on our desk, and there were pictures hung up and an exhibit of our Social Studies, a science exhibit, and pictures in the hall. Miff's class had folders, pictures up, a few branches fastened to make a tree, and on the branches were birds and butterflies they made. . . . Please come home,
Love, Julie

(May 25, 1968, to Mrs. Blanche Collins at Connecticut Valley Hospital)

My mother remained at Connecticut Valley Hospital for well over a year, missing many more school events, holidays, birthdays, and other milestones of childhood. In the time she was away I went from a little to a big girl. I was one of the tallest kids in my class and my grades were the highest. My hair grew long and straggly, my clothes too short and tight. I acquired a new awkwardness, in which shyness and reticence butted up against uneasiness about the motives of others.

My father and grandmother's strained relationship worsened. With Mom gone, and all her valuable domestic skills, my grandmother saw her son's faults more starkly and regretted the harsh judgments she'd directed at her struggling daughter-in-law. Stung by his mother's disapproval, Dad started clamming up in her company or leaving the room.

At first he did his best to keep our family going, focusing on Miff and me because we were more malleable and forgiving than the sons he'd let down so often. One evening he took just us girls to the Schubert Theater in New Haven to see *Desert Flower*, our first play. Dad was utterly delighted when we spotted the leading lady at the pricey restaurant where we dined after the performance on roast beef, Idaho baked potatoes, and hot apple pie—I remember the menu because it was one of Dad's favorite meals. He got the star to autograph our program, and was so proud when he came back and pointed out her scrawled message.

I doubt I showed much enthusiasm for our historic night on the town, or for any of the rare outings Dad managed. He quickly gave up, consumed by his own worries. His sales commissions, already meager, were falling off. Nervousness corroded his temper. Sometimes his laugh made me think of a barking, angry dog. He stayed away more, arriving home later than necessary. Sometimes he ordered his daughters to bed early, and I could tell he simply wanted to be rid of our taxing, needful presence.

Left to our own devices my sister and I floundered and began to look the part of neglected children. Our hair went uncombed and our clothes became ragged, fastened together with strategic pins and knots. When Jennifer lost a shoe sole Dad drove her back to school so they could hunt for it because there was no money to buy her a new pair. During recess one day, the elastic I'd knotted broke and my underpants fell down on the playground in the middle of a crowd of kids. They teased me mercilessly, spreading the news that Julie's panties were full of holes.

Our health also deteriorated. We had frequent toothaches. We daubed our sore, abscessed gums with oil of clove, an Augy remedy. I regularly came down with bronchitis and tonsillitis, losing my voice for a week at a time so Dad sent me to school with notes: "Please don't call on Julie today in class. She has laryngitis again and can't talk." Then my grades slumped because I couldn't see the blackboard clearly. The school intervened, checked my eyes, and paid for a pair of glasses, a well-intended humiliation.

As I muddled along, I relied more than ever on Stacey's friendship. She didn't seem so eager to be with me, however. Something was up; I could tell from the hardening of her manner toward me, her sneering reactions to things I said. She used to love coming to my house until my mother discouraged it, but even with Mom out of the picture she never suggested it any more. One weekend afternoon, when we were hanging out with some of the other Collins Drive kids, Stacey made her move. She flicked those strange-colored eyes my way and announced to the group, "Hey, do you guys know Mrs. Collins is an ALKA-HALL-LICK?" She savored her big new word. "That means she's a drunk. My mother said she can't stop drinking so they locked her up in a mental hospital." The other kids didn't know how to react and stayed quiet, which didn't satisfy Stacey. Changing tactics, she took ruthless aim at me. "Hey everybody, look at what Julie's wearing today—EWWWW! She had almost the same thing on yesterday. I bet she only changes once a week. I'll tell you something else, too. She's deaf in one ear." She raised her voice, pointing. "It's all deformed and weird looking. I'll show you—" she went to brush my hair aside with her grubby fingers, to reveal the secret I'd never entrusted to any friend but her. The other kids moved closer, curious to see. I lurched backward, one loud sob escaping before I could stop it.

"Oh my God, what a baby!" Stacey exulted. I opened my mouth to protest. "Baby! Baby!" my best friend taunted.

"Quit it, Stacey! You—you—dirty pismire!" Pismire was one of my father's fancy words. I wasn't sure what it meant, except it was bad. Before she could regain the upper hand I bolted and ran back to her house to get my things. Mrs. Ketchum was there. She asked what was wrong but I knew she didn't care. I hated her and her daughter. I stumbled home, bawling myself blind, knowing I couldn't tell Dad what had happened. I never set foot inside the Ketchum's house again.

Stacey's betrayal left a big hole. My sister had made some close buddies and spent the after-school hours at their houses. Cut off from Stacey and her Collins Drive gang, I had nobody my age nearby. Two older girls who had been nice to me had gone off to junior high and a wider social circle that included boys. My current school was in a different part of town and my classmates didn't live nearby. Weekly library books became my dear companions. I gravitated toward those published decades ago, about characters and settings that bore no resemblance to my world. When I got off the bus each afternoon I rushed upstairs to my room to forget myself in their fragrant, delicately browning pages.

With time to burn I took on more tasks to assist my dad—folding the laundry, sweeping floors, making breakfast on school mornings for my sister and me. My specialties were lumpy Cream of Wheat, leathery scrambled eggs, and weepy French toast. I packed our lunches too: bologna for Miff and Fluffernutter sandwiches for me. I also took to telling Mom about my sister's doings since Miff was too young to be a reliable correspondent. I mentioned a bully who was bothering her, noted her coughs and fevers. One morning Miff started sobbing at the bus stop because it was bitter cold out and, like Dad, we never dressed warmly enough. I dutifully passed this information to Mom too, but mostly I censored the bleaker aspects of our lives, knowing she could or would do nothing in response.

While Mom was gone I had my First Communion, receiving that pasty white wafer on my tongue while decked out in white, from veil to shoes. I also went to Confession regularly, where I made up sins to confess to the faceless murmuring priest in the booth, thinking it was my Catholic duty to rack up enough bad deeds to be fined at least a Hail Mary and some rosary bead recitations. I no longer prayed, however. At first I only skipped a night or two before my conscience elbowed me, admonishing, better pray for Mom, better pray for Dad! It didn't take long, though, till I gave up praying for good. I was angry with God. I went from thinking I might grow up to be a nun and arguing creationism with my brother Peter, already an avowed atheist and scientific thinker, to shunning God altogether in private. When I stared up at my bedroom ceiling I no longer imagined a portal opening to heaven, where His listening ear was turned to my whispering voice. I saw the cracks and furrowed plaster of a weakening ceiling, and nothing more. I was becoming like my father. He thought prayer was a waste of time too.

Soon after my friendship with Stacey busted up, I realized Mrs. Ketchum was definitely out of the picture. I'd been slow to pick up on the fact that the midnight meetings and beach-blanket rendezvous had all stopped. So my father was no longer Pine Orchard's dashing Lothario. Neither was he the cheerful, outgoing neighbor and family man of days gone by. He was a loner now, a frowning, too-thin middle-aged man in a tired suit who carried a battered briefcase and drove a second-hand wagon in search of an elusive prosperity. He was also the only parent I had and I clung to him.

I had lost track of my father's resume long ago, but even I could tell he was growing seriously discouraged. He never talked about the future anymore. That Memorial Day when I was eight was the first time he didn't trot out his Marine uniform. It stayed in his wardrobe thereafter, retired from duty. We went to the parade as usual and he chain-smoked through the festivities, an uneasy, distracted bystander. He tolerated our pleas for souvenirs and treats, but his only interest in the day was to stand by the World War II memorial lost in thought, littering the ground with butts while Miff and I entertained each other and kept out of his way.

Gradually I adapted to the stark realities of home. I perked up and developed some spunk. To hell with Stacey and her cronies—I was fine on my own. I went to the town carnival all by myself where I rode the two or three scary rides and visited the fortuneteller, who disappointed me with the dull promise of a handsome husband and lots of kids. I took long walks in the woods, bringing a book along. I rode my bike past the Hotchkiss Grove beaches and on to Indian Neck, whizzing by the street where my Aunt Alice and Uncle Bill lived, whom I never saw now, around the hairpin turn, and on to the salt marsh. I always stopped there to gaze at the seawater carving escape routes among the undulating grasses. Then I headed back to Hotchkiss Grove where I prowled the sand, shedding my shoes and socks. I sat on the rocks and stared out at the Thimble Islands.

The day Mom checked out of Connecticut Valley for good she brought along the tile mosaic ashtrays, ceramic figures, sock monkeys, and crocheted slippers, potholders, and unfinished afghan she'd made in the hospital craft class. When she arrived at 101 PO she looked wan and scrawny in her old dress. But her lost expression and beaten-down manner were gone. Instead she exuded an alarming purposefulness, her old self amplified and with a hard new edge. Rushing to her I was giddy with relief. "You're back, you're back, you're back!" "Julie, darling!" Her huge smile, the confident grip of her arms assured me that all would be okay. This time she'd stay put. We were a family again! I was so elated that I forgot all about my father. He must have picked her up and driven her home, but he doesn't figure at all in my memories of the reunion.

Very soon I found out what was driving my mother's worrisome intensity, and why my father seemed to vanish the moment she re-entered our lives. Along with sobriety Mom had acquired an ironclad conviction. Her marriage was over. She had spurned Dad's pleas for reconciliation and, with his mother's blessing, ordered him out of the house.

He took off quietly. There were no good-byes. So I regained one parent and lost the other. The joy of having Mom back turned into anxiety as she threw herself into parenting and household matters with frightening zeal. I wasn't sure if she would last. At night I pricked up my ears to catch the sounds that would tell me she was drinking again.

And I missed my sad-faced father. How could he manage alone? I found out he'd moved into a shabby hotel in Indian Neck. He began dropping by on Saturdays, to take Miff and me out for the afternoon. He was shaving erratically, I noticed, so that his cheek scoured mine when he kissed me hello. That eighty-proof bouquet was back and the whites of his eyes looked hard-boiled. He seemed perpetually exhausted too. I thought of him pacing some strange room in the middle of the night, pursued by his dark thoughts with no daughters to distract or comfort him.

These observations plus our awful attempts at normalcy when he took us to consume some unwanted treat made me dread his visits. One Saturday I finally lost it, pitching a wild emotional fit, weeping and banging on things while Dad waited for me to come downstairs. I heard somebody explain that I didn't want to go, which made me bawl all the harder, for now my poor dad knew I hated being with him. He finally left with Miff and without me. Once I calmed down I felt guilty but also relieved. I had discovered my only effective weapon, unpredictable anger, which revived my old nickname "Stormcloud" and began to frighten my daddy away; I was no longer his little girl, his adoring fan, and now he and I both knew it.

*　*　*

The only good Jap is a dead Jap.

(US World War II propaganda)

The only aspect of the Okinawa invasion Dad talked about readily was the April action. His whole speaking style changed, becoming animated and passionate when he described how fast the Marines moved and how much of the island they captured single-handedly. "Two-thirds!" he exclaimed, as if the feat had happened yesterday. "You should have seen us, Chule. Your ole dad was fast on his feet back then, and we were carrying heavy packs that weighed half as much as we did."

Of course, with the bulk of Japanese forces to the south the Marines were able to make short work of the north, so Dad's "two-thirds!" claim didn't tell the whole story. Nonetheless, his boast never rang hollow to me because it meant something precious to him—that the Marines were unstoppable, the elite among fighting men. And so had been the young Jerry Collins who gamely charged alongside his brethren, always keeping up, never slacking off.

In some ways, my father told me, Okinawa was a pleasant surprise—at first. The subtropical climate was less oppressive than that of fetid Guadalcanal now thousands of miles to the south, where he had contracted a couple of persistent infections requiring hospitalization. Okinawa's season of torrential rain, monsoon surges, and typhoons hadn't begun yet, and he found the abandoned rice paddies and terraced fields an incongruously peaceful sight.

My dad enjoyed reliving those April weeks when he and the boys were in peak physical condition and ripping across the north. The Marines were living on K rations by then, he explained, a menu of canned hash and eggs or pork and beans plus "beak-bender" biscuits and candy bars that didn't melt. Beverages were soluble coffee or "battery acid," a sickening lemony drink. K rations were eaten on the line. The more palatable C rations were eaten while in reserve. My sister and I thought the Ks and Cs sounded like great fun, a wartime picnic of sorts. That irked Dad, who made a point of telling us how the men lost their appetites during combat, subsisting on coffee, chewing gum, and smokes. "Usually, the rations they gave us were a couple of years old. We'd open the cans and the food was spoilt or moldy." The hamburgerlike patties Miff and I fed to Dan our dachshund were far more appetizing than the Marines' cuisine, he said.

Like my father I had great stamina but scant athletic prowess. He'd had a talent for basketball, at least, but I was lousy at any and all team sports. It bothered him that I was turning into a dank mushroom, rooted indoors with my books. He often would try to nag me into activity by contrasting my soft life with his rough-and-ready days on the march and long nights hunkered down in a fox-hole. "We dug the holes ourselves, with an entrenching tool," he said. "About eighteen inches deep. It seemed like we were digging our own graves each night. When it rained our foxholes filled and turned into mud at the bottom. Imagine having to sleep in that muck with rain beating on your helmet. What a dog's life we led. We'd listen to the big guns, the shelling going on all around and try to figure out how close they'd hit. You never stuck your head out to look, though, because the Japs would blow it right off."

Any Marine who left his foxhole at night to pee could be mis-taken for an enemy infiltrator and shot by one of his own. "We were all afraid of infiltrators. They crawled in carrying grenades. When they got close enough they tossed one into the nearest fox-hole. If somebody tried to stop them, they'd pull the grenade clip and blow up with it, martyring themselves for their Emperor. Sometimes they jumped right into the hole with a knife or bayonet. Just knowing they were out there made it impossible to sleep more than a few winks at a time."

My dad always told me more about his war than he ought, and the accounts grew increasingly graphic as I became a better listener, transfixed by horrors far worse than any of those Creature Features Stacey and I used to watch. He told me about scouting missions when he came upon American bodies with smashed skulls, the brains removed, and sand poured into the empty cavity by the enemy, or bodies with their abdomens sliced open and innards pulled out. "The Japs were sending us a message," he said grimly. "To them we were nothing but beasts." He described various tortures the enemy was notorious for using on living men till I begged him to stop.

At such times I could feel an old, conditioned hatred flicker in my dad. Young Jerry Collins had shared the widespread American notion, bolstered by propaganda, that only the Japanese committed the atrocities in the Pacific. Yet he also observed evidence of brutality on his side. He told me about spotting bodies of Okinawans, women and children, who'd been killed by American troops, and surrendering Japanese who were gunned down by angry combat vets. There were rapes, too, although he was circumspect on that topic with his daughter. He also told me about the souvenir hunters. It was common for US fighting men to strip Japanese corpses of banzai swords, uniforms, and other personal effects, for souvenirs to impress the folks back home. The more ghoulish went further still, removing gold fillings and teeth, even ears.

During one patrol my father and his partner spotted a GI who had been gravely wounded while attempting to strip some enemy bodies. That was as stupid as you could get—harvesting grotesque mementos out in the open while snipers took leisurely aim. The poor idiot was in terrible shape, and Dad and his patrol partner rushed in and carried him to the nearest aid station. The souvenir hunter died on the way, one of countless pointless and ugly deaths my father would witness before his war was over.

As I later found out, the dead Okinawans, the raped women, and the mortally wounded souvenir hunter weren't mentioned in Dad's letters home. Nor was one of his worst moments in the war, when a face-to-face encounter with a Japanese soldier undermined his faith in himself as a Marine.

Like many of my father's Okinawa memories, this one is hard to pinpoint in time and space. I later learned that combat veterans often cannot remember precisely when or where their experiences occurred. The gore and clamor of war freezes some memories, even banal ones, into crystal clarity, while tangling and blurring others. I do know Dad's company was heading south to join the assault on the Shuri Line, the backbone of General Ushijima's defense forces, when he was sent out on a routine patrol. Usually the men went in pairs but for some reason Dad was alone when he heard something behind him and whirled around, his rifle ready.

A Japanese soldier stared back at him, no more than three or four yards away. It was common for Marine scouts to run into members of the Okinawan home guard while on patrol, and these poorly armed and trained men, conscripted by the Japanese, never posed much of a threat. In fact, Dad had already met a few locals on friendly terms. He'd helped escort some Okinawans to safety when they were too close to a combat zone, and a few men in his unit had even risked their lives doing the same under friendly fire. So he had already seen enough Okinawans to recognize their smaller, rounder faces and forms. Besides, his training had included memorizing the Japanese military hierarchy and uniforms, and he knew that the soldier eyeballing him now not only was Japanese but also a member of a crack division.

Both men faced an enemy gun aimed at their vitals. Both were frozen into position, poised to shoot. Dad's highly trained reflexes should have clicked in automatically, he said. Likewise the other man's, and at least one of them should have fallen right to the ground, dead or gravely wounded. Instead my father only stood there, gaping at the slight figure at least half a foot shorter than he, who appeared much younger than twenty-two-year-old Jerry Collins. "He was a little guy. I could have sworn he was sixteen, tops. Just a kid," Dad said. "Though for all I know he was thirty. We were as motionless as two stones, except for breathing. But I got a good look at his eyes and he was as scared as I was."

So, in theory and according to propaganda, on one side was the US Marine, standing in for American values of patriotism, courage, and self-sacrifice. On the other was the Japanese soldier, honoring righteousness, duty to the Emperor, and *bushido*, the code of the warrior. In reality, two young, quaking strangers faced off on alien soil, deposited there by forces over which they had no control.

On some inexplicable impulse my father turned on his heels and began to stride away from the enemy soldier, tensing in anticipation of a bullet to the back. He dared a quick glance over his shoulder and was astounded to see his nemesis was also retreating. In fact, the Japanese soldier burst into a run, inspiring my father to instantly follow suit, though heading in the opposite direction. This is ridiculous, he thought. A US Marine, bolting like a bunny. "I knew I looked like an idiot. I started laughing so hard I got a cramp and had to stop running. By then the other guy was completely out of sight."

The first time I heard this story, it bothered me a lot. What was there to laugh about? Dad should have killed that soldier! Instead he ran away. Was my father a coward, then, instead of the brave fighter I'd always imagined? Why did he let the bad guy go? Wasn't war supposed to be a straightforward business of kill or be killed? Especially World War II, when Americans and their allies were fighting to save the world from the Nazis who murdered the Jews in ovens and the Japs who liked to pull peoples' fingernails off?

"You should have shot him, Dad." I ventured. "Shouldn't you?"

"Of course I should have!" My father was instantly upset. "But I couldn't do it. That soldier wasn't what I expected. He was a scared little pipsqueak. I don't think he was even shaving yet. He didn't look like he could hurt anyone."

"Then maybe it's good you didn't shoot," I said, trying to lighten things up.

He sucked in his breath and held it, glaring at me. For a weird moment I wondered if he wanted to hit me. "Appearances are deceiving, Julie. He looked harmless, but he was a highly trained soldier. And because of me, he got another chance to kill people. Maybe even buddies of mine."

I didn't say, "Well, his letting you live meant you could kill people too." I was too nervous to argue. When I was older and heard this story again, I commended him for holding his fire and walking away, rejecting the role of killing machine when he could. "That's a load of crap," he snapped, deeply offended. "It was my job to shoot him. I let my buddies down."

And because he didn't shoot that day, Jerry Collins felt compelled to use his rifle as soon as possible, to counter what he considered an act of cowardice and prove to himself he was a worthy Marine. While all the men in his reconnaissance outfit were proficient riflemen, their primary mission was to scout the enemy and report back, not to kill. In fact, many combat veterans never got around to shooting because they were too busy dashing and dropping to the ground. That wasn't the case with Dad. He did fire his M-1, though he would never say how often or how accurate a marksman he proved to be. As an adult I was bold enough to ask him, point blank, how many men he'd killed. "Oh, a few, I suppose," he said, looking at me funny, as if he didn't trust me and wondered why the hell I would ask. "It was hard to tell for sure, under the circumstances."

The only time I recall him letting any details slip out was in the intensive care unit toward the end of his life, when he raved that the Japs were coming to get him because he'd just killed two of theirs. But was that his memory resurfacing, or a hallucination? For all this Marine's frankness, for all the raw moments when the old grief, fear, and pride rushed out of him, my father clammed up completely when it came to the topic of him taking lives.

CHAPTER EIGHT

JERRY ALONE

1-4 TAKING OF SUGAR LOAF HILL – VICINITY OF NAHA

A postcard from Jerry Collins of Sugar Loaf Hill

Marines on their seventh [it was actually the fourteenth] attempt to capture sanguinary Sugar Loaf Hill, key to Naha and the Asato corridor to Shuri, were in firm control of the crest and were moving slowly down the reverse slope today, while tanks slaughtered hundreds of Japanese fleeing from tombs and caves midway down the slope. Sugar Loaf Hill will go down in history as one of the most desperate and costly actions of the Pacific war.

(New York Herald Tribune, *Sunday, May 20, 1945*)

As the radio and the newspapers have probably told you we have had quite a time for ourselves here on this rock. The Nips seem determined to fight to the last man so it seems we'll have to clean them all up. [Our] regiment had a tough assignment and from what I can see the second battalion hit the roughest job when they gave us Sugar Loaf Hill to take.... It has been costly these past six or seven days but I believe the Japs are losing their hold now.... Our section has had its share of casualties.... We are back in reserve now and resting up a little. The rest is a big help as the boys are out of range of most of the shelling and all the whistles are our own shells. We call it "outgoing mail."

(*May 21, two days after the Marines captured Sugar Loaf Hill*)

A few years ago, when I became obsessed with one week in 1945, I found among Dad's letters an antique black-and-white military-issue postcard depicting a scorched and blackened mound labeled Sugar Loaf Hill. On the back Pfc. Collins had tersely inked: "We attacked from this side and our battalion lost it 3 or 4 times before holding it. Loomis was killed here with about half the outfit as casualties."

In May 1945 Dad's regiment, the Twenty-ninth, took a lead role in the seven-day assault to seize an insignificant-looking lump on the Okinawan landscape. But Sugar Loaf would prove to be the bloodiest island battle of the Pacific, far worse than even Iwo Jima. It ultimately left more than 80 percent of the Twenty-ninth regiment dead and survivors, including my father, branded for life by the ordeal. I studied that postcard for a while, imagining him as a young Marine racing up the slope.

Only when Dad became persona non grata in our family did he talk frankly about his experience on Sugar Loaf. In the bleakest period of his postwar life, when he was forty-eight and I was eleven, his memories seized on the worst of his war, when a sweetly named hill became deadly ground. In what was also my unhappiest time, as my dad slipped out of reach, a single week in 1945 pulled us together.

But first my family shattered then reassembled in a precarious new form.

One November afternoon, in 1968, Mom arrived home in a strangely agitated state. She'd been gone all morning conducting some mysterious "business." Dressed in her Sunday clothes, she said she had something important to tell my sister and me. "My marriage to your father is over," was her blunt announcement. "I'm getting a divorce. You kids should know that divorce goes against everything I believe in. But his behavior left me no other choice. He's still your father, however, and he will always love you very, very much."

That's how the bomb finally hit, wiping out my family for good. Dad wasn't around when it happened. I began to weep while Mom described her appearance before a judge. How could she sound so remote and calm? I'd had no idea she'd been in court that day. My parents hadn't warned us this might happen. I'd kept on hoping Dad would charm his way back into Mom's good graces. I thought of the master bedroom and couldn't remember when they'd last shared it. The concept of divorce was unfamiliar and unsettling. As far as I knew, my parents were the first couple in our neighborhood to blast "till death do us part" to smithereens.

Within days of receiving this news, I was buying candy on Main Street, at the shop I usually avoided because the couple who owned it suspected every kid of having sticky fingers, curtly hustling us in and out so we couldn't stuff our pockets. As I paid for my penny candy the husband gave me a sharp look. "Kid, what's your name?"

"Julie Collins."

"Your father Jerry Collins?"

I nodded, instantly wary of the white-haired man behind the counter.

"You poor Collins, poor kid," he muttered sympathetically, shaking his head, dropping coins into my palm. He said something else but I couldn't make out his accented English, other than "drinking."

"Shut up! Shut up! Don't you say that!" I shook my fist at him and stormed out of the shop. Then I walked my bike nearly the whole way home, too upset to ride. I was torn between fury and grief. What gave that man, who was practically a stranger, the right to bad-mouth my dad? It felt as though my innards were exposed for anybody to tromp on.

Soon after my parents split up for good Mom went to a hairdresser and had her thick mane chopped off. The severe Prince Valiant cut announced that the old Blanche who had aspired to Jackie O. elegance and *Woman's Day* domestic flair was kaput. The new Blanche seemed eager to embrace a chaste and Catholic middle age, to concentrate on getting a job, paying the bills, and tending to her children. She somehow paid for a battery of dental visits and medical checkups for Miff and me. Then she enrolled in driving school and applied for whatever employment a woman with a housewife's resume could get. In desperation she would take one crummy job after another: telemarketing, factory work, housecleaning, assisting an elderly woman, clerking at a health food store, and substitute teaching. Now she was the functioning parent and Dad was the falling-down drunk.

His initial stay at the decrepit Waverly Hotel in Indian Neck was followed by a stint in detox, though I didn't know about that until later on. He simply vanished for a while. Then he took up residence at another dive, in New Haven, still drinking heavily. He stopped working completely and our financial situation at home became dire. Mom had planned for us to leave the Collins homestead and find an apartment elsewhere in town but now that was out of the question—much to my relief. Even though my grandmother, then in her seventies, depended on Mom to run the house and made concessions to keep her there, she was very protective of her bank accounts. Too proud to seek help from her siblings, Mom signed up for welfare and food stamps. I shrank inside whenever she took out those telltale coupon books at the supermarket checkout, but at least she was striving, not giving up like Dad.

I grew accustomed to erratic gaps in communication with him. Weeks sometimes went by with no word. Occasionally he mailed letters from New Haven to Miff and me, written in code. In the past he had told us about World War II code-cracking operations and demonstrated simple coding. The gibberish he sent instead of conventional fatherly communications drove us crazy. Perhaps he intended a playful game but it smacked of desperation, a cry for help. Years later my sister recalled how she couldn't decipher what our father wrote and was consumed with guilt for failing. I never even tried to break his dumb code. Why couldn't my dad write me in a normal way, for crying out loud? Somewhere I have a couple of those letters stashed away, their contents still unknown.

The divorce was final in April 1969. Dad continued to wallow while Mom desperately scrimped and trolled the want ads. Hoping to improve her prospects, she enrolled in typing and stenography classes. Our rudderless state kept all of us on edge. When Patrick set off for college next, it hit me that he and Jeremiah had left home for good, their grown-up lives steaming off in independent directions. Now the man of the house was my youngest brother Peter, who became our overburdened anchor. He worked shifts at the local wire mill, in restaurant kitchens, and finally as a prized employee at Collins & Freeman on Main Street, the hardware store our grandfather Pop had once owned.

It soon became clear that neither of my parents could make it on their own, even with Peter helping Mom financially. She decided to let her ex-husband come back to live with us, so he could get back on his feet and start paying child support and alimony. When Dad returned to 101 PO after many months away, it was to sleep alone in the nursery my sister and I once shared. He had lost Mom's love and forfeited his place in the family. His own mother had shifted her loyalty to his ex-wife. Regardless, he seemed relieved to be back in his childhood home, to stand in the driveway watching the sun dip behind the enormous oaks and evergreens that were already venerable when he was a boy.

He began to go through the motions of making a living again, and drank less. For a while my parents cautiously circled around each other, getting used to the new lay of the land. I became a feverishly dedicated fifth grader at the Indian Neck School, craving day-to-day stability and routine away from my fractured family.

My teacher was a gruff, tough-talking New Yorker named Mr. Grosh, who commuted four hours round-trip every day to teach us Branford yokels. Ethical behavior was a favorite topic of his and he quizzed our class regularly on hypothetical misbehaviors to firm up our moral makeup. Mr. Grosh also had a trove of cautionary tales of reckless children who licked metal flagpoles in winter or, disobediently dashing through school hallways, lost eyeballs on the locker doors left ajar by other careless students. He shared with the class his moneymaking schemes to plant groves of prized black walnut trees or sell used tires to East Asia for recycling into sandals. Every day at noon he sent a student to the cafeteria to fetch his carton of buttermilk, which he poured into a glass and chugged in front of us, praising its healthful qualities. Many classmates found him weird and occasionally terrifying. Not I. I thought Mr. Grosh was wonderful. Eccentric to be sure, but a powerful character, a dedicated teacher, and, at bottom, a sensitive man who focused on me at a time when my own dad had given up fathering. Mr. Grosh wrote gung-ho notes on my tests and homework, gave me special assignments, and bestowed small marks of favor. He told me frequently, with kindly ferocity, that I was worthy of "grrr-REAT expectations."

To show his confidence in me, he appointed me monitor for the special-ed class that gathered each morning before the bell at the far end of the playground. Initially I was upset to be singled out and separated from my classmates. I was also frightened of the special-ed kids, especially Rusty, a huge, red-haired boy who sometimes got into fights I had to break up, and Donna, a boisterous, heavy-set girl with Down's Syndrome who hunted me down for a daily lung-squashing hug. I adapted, however, and my experience shepherding these kids helped snap me out of self-absorption. The rest of the school teased and scorned the special-ed students. Clearly, they faced a far rougher future than did a run-of-the-mill misfit like me. By the end of that school year I had grown fond of my charges. Years later, when I heard that Mr. Grosh had died in an auto accident while commuting, I mourned a kind man who saw that Julie Collins was more than a "poor kid" and pushed me to step out of myself.

That year I did shed some of my solitary ways. Two girls in my class started asking me over after school. I didn't reciprocate, however, fearful my new friends would discover the strange truth about my parents. I particularly dreaded the question: "What does your father do?" I also didn't join Girl Scouts and made excuses to skip group activities, such as skating parties and swim clubs, which always involved parents. I wasn't entirely left out, though, because I tried hard to be friendly otherwise. Sometimes I got invited to birthday parties where I joined for the first time in the preteen games of spin the bottle and post office. I also developed a passion for a good-natured, outgoing boy named Rick who regularly asked me to be his square dance partner.

While I tentatively established my own social life, my parents were warring again. Mom had chosen to live under the same roof with her ex-husband, calling it "a business arrangement." But the arrangement wasn't working out. Dad's financial contributions were sporadic and inadequate, stoking her deep resentment.

I'm sure my father dreaded coming home at night. He often stopped at a bar along the way and came into the house red eyed and scotch scented, which inevitably unleashed Mom's fury. In a breathtaking distortion of reality, she attended Al-Anon meetings for family members of alcoholics and badgered him to go to Alcoholics Anonymous meetings—for the ones with the REAL problem. Dad drank his way through depressions, but his sloppy benders never approached the devastating force of her addiction. Mom had left Connecticut Valley a dry drunk. She remained sober through sheer willpower and blamed her drinking history entirely on Dad, which added an unbearable dishonesty to their fights. I began escaping to my room or else left the house the moment Mom and Dad raised their voices.

Then a pitiful episode made me reach out to my father again. After a particularly nasty blowup with Mom he quietly slipped out the next morning, leaving a message lying in full view on the table, clearly intending for any or all of us to see it. It wound up in my hands. I remember the gist of the first part: "Blanche, I can't go on like this. Life has become a living hell. I know I've screwed up every-thing. You would all be better off without me."

The rest I couldn't bring myself to read. That despairing note sent me into a tailspin. Was my father threatening to kill himself? Somebody, Mom perhaps, took the note and reassured me it was nothing more than a bid for sympathy. The idea of Jerry Collins doing himself in was ludicrous. He wasn't capable of so decisive an act. He'd lost all credibility.

I knew that was so, and calmed down. He was still my father, however, and I couldn't stand his lonely suffering. I started keeping a close eye on him. It hurt to see his looks wearing away, his glossy hair dull, his eyes perpetually bloodshot, and his fastidious elegance long gone. Always whippet thin, he had grown emaciated. I'd learned about tapeworms in my science class and I worried my dad had one inside him taking all the nourishment. I baked the cakes and cookies he liked, hoping he would gain weight. I tried to be kinder, to hide my impatience with his depression and inertia. Instead of avoiding Dad, I began to seek his company. When he stood outside smoking I joined him, nervous and shy, kicking at the gravel while I waited for the heavy silence to lift.

* * *

The newspapers were fairly accurate on the Sugar Loaf story and it was pretty rough. Since then we've hit several tough spots and have been in a few precarious positions but that was tops. The best thing about this section is the ability of the boys to retain their sense of humor, which has seen us through when many of our closest buddies have been killed. Later, I believe, is when we shall miss them most. However, they are gone and there is nothing we can do.

(June 17, 1945)

As I entered sixth grade the escalating fighting in Vietnam pushed World War II deeper into the past. A product of my era, I grew my hair long, burned incense, and dressed in "hippie" styles. I wore a huge smiley-face pin and a peace symbol pendant. I decorated the brown paper covers I put on my schoolbooks with more peace symbols and doves with olive branches in their beaks and *Make Love Not War* spelled out in groovy curvy letters. I tie-dyed T-shirts and painted some pants with the same motifs. I became a Dylan fan. But even while I followed the news about antiwar demonstrations and village massacres, and worried about my brothers and the draft, underneath I was just like my dad—fixated on an old conflict already fought and ended.

All the attention focused on Vietnam aggravated my father. He was against that war but he despised antiwar arguments that seemed to implicate all veterans in immoral acts. "Our war was different," he insisted. It also bothered him that the savagery of the Pacific war had been forgotten. The brutal chaos of Vietnam, the napalm attacks and burning bodies, the elusive enemy escaping via underground tunnels, the civilians caught in the middle all brought back memories of June 12 to June 19, 1945.

It is during this period that Dad told me about Sugar Loaf for the first time. We were sitting in the playroom, which Mom had turned into a sewing room. She was out of the house. My sister was nearby, perhaps listening in too. Dad began his account in a matter-of-fact way, but I remember how I held my breath from the suspense. His demeanor tipped me off—he didn't look at Miff or me as he talked. He only looked into the past.

In April 1945, while his Sixth Marine Division cruised up north on Okinawa, the Army had knocked itself out trying to smash General Ushijima's superb defenses in the south. For weeks the Army divisions led by General Simon Buckner suffered heavy losses gaining minimal ground. Meanwhile, escalating kamikaze assaults harried the naval support forces. In early May the Sixth Marines were ordered south to relieve the Army's mediocre Twenty-seventh Infantry

Division on the front lines. The Twenty-seventh in turn took the Sixth's place up north. General Buckner now turned his Tenth Army supported by the Marines to the job of smashing the enemy's main defense, the Shuri Line. The Sixth Division was to hit this line— which they referred to as the Machinato Line—on the west, pushing down the coast to outflank the Japanese stronghold at the ancient Shuri Castle, and press on toward Naha, the island capital.

Anchoring the western end of this line was a hill, flanked by two smaller hills. Dad never told me the actual size of Sugar Loaf; I assumed it had to be huge. In fact, it was only three hundred yards long and about one hundred feet high. However, this nearly barren bump, curiously nicknamed by the Marines, would prove diabolically lethal. Sugar Loaf and its neighbors Horseshoe and Half Moon, a.k.a. Crescent, were riddled with tiered tunnels and caves and pockmarked with camouflaged openings and gun emplacements. The hills stood in an open plain, so any advance would come under direct fire. The tunnels connecting hill to hill meant the Japanese officers could swiftly shift troops to meet attacks as needed. And whenever the Marines stormed up Sugar Loaf, Japanese soldiers could emerge from protected positions on the reverse slope to pounce on the attackers. "We were sitting ducks," Dad said.

By then the Twenty-ninth had a new commander, Col. William Whaling. The Second Battalion commander was Lt. Col. William Robb. Despite Dad's disdain for officers in general, he thought pretty well of Whaling and Robb. However, the men he felt really deserved respect were the infantry, regular guys like himself who were ordered to throw themselves at Sugar Loaf and its sisters at any cost. "Fight to the last man," he said. "Julie, do you understand what that means?"

I nodded.

On May 12 the first Marine rifle company to attempt the dash lost most of its men. Many other companies were clobbered as

Sugar Loaf changed hands more than a dozen times. My father's worst days of the war began on May 14 when he was assigned as a scout-observer to a rifle company—Dog Company, I believe—on the front line. Despite some combat experience en route to Sugar Loaf he was still unnerved by his earlier face-off with a Japanese soldier. For all he knew, that very man was hiding in the slope ahead. Much of the time the Marines couldn't see the enemy darting from its superbly camouflaged positions. At one point my father heard Japanese shouts beneath his feet as soldiers moved through a tunnel. "My hair stood on end," he recalled.

A military photographer shot some footage of Dad running up Sugar Loaf to lay communication wires, so he could radio headquarters. Some time after the battle he saw himself on film. Those seconds of footage document his earliest moments on the hill, and the last captured with any clarity. From here on I have to assemble his story from numerous tellings since it came out differently each time. This was not because he altered the facts but because his memories of what happened during subsequent days were scrambled, flashing with bits of scenes and faces so excruciatingly vivid they brought tears to his eyes while I listened.

At the front line my father entered a howling world of explosions and screams, with bullets and mortars and shards of metal flying all about, flesh-eating goo raining from phosphorous shells, and anti-aircraft fire weaving a net across the sky. On Sugar Loaf the enemy seemed to hurl its entire arsenal at once, and the American counterattack was equally lethal to Marines caught in the open at the wrong place and time.

Almost immediately Dad witnessed the most appalling degradation of the human body imaginable. He'd already seen plenty of casualties, but his reaction had been muted by the Marines' efficient retrieval of the bodies. On Sugar Loaf the steel torrent of enemy artillery tore off limbs and heads, gouged eyes, seared flesh, and sliced men in half. Intestines spilled from exploded chest cavities. Marines flew into the air and landed in pieces. Unidentifiable chunks of flesh were scattered everywhere. American and Japanese corpses piled up quickly, in obscene disarray. It was impossible to evacuate most of the dead Marines and they quickly decayed in the humid heat. The stench of putrefying flesh quivering with maggots was inescapable.

The shrieking horrors sickened and isolated Dad—one little speck in the midst of mayhem. He had counted on the Marine skills and instincts drilled into him to see him through. It didn't take long, however, for the grisly idiocy of the situation to make survival seem a ridiculous game of chance. The lack of cover turned Sugar Loaf into a shooting gallery. The Marines' jungle training was of little use on the naked slopes. There was no way to protect one-self or prepare for this kind of killing. The frenzied fighting turned him into a mass of nerve endings, raw terror alternating with vacant numbness. What scared him most was the unexpected solitude as he raced about trying to do his job—relaying information, carrying messages, reporting coordinates, taking occasional aim at the elusive enemy.

Time after time the Marines gained a foothold on the hill only to be shot to pieces. The last two days of fighting were the worst. Okinawa's rainy season had turned the pitted red clay earth into an open cesspool. Prone to respiratory and other infections, Dad suffered in the constant wet from dysentery and foot ailments. The Japanese pulled in some fresh recruits and fought with intensified fervor, determined to crush the Marines' spirit before their own grave losses forced withdrawal.

Dad's hottest moments came when his rifle company made another futile charge for the summit. That night he lay by himself in a wet shell hole, where he kept an eye out for infiltrators. The constant noise, the pounding and squealing of shells and artillery punctured by screaming and wailing in English and Japanese made it impossible to think or rest. His tired eyes ached from staring hard into the dark. He began to hallucinate moving shapes and flashes of light, a constant unintelligible murmuring. At one point he was sure he heard Pop calling, "Jerry, over here!" and nearly climbed out of his hole. Some sensible instinct fortunately held him back. No harm came to him that night, but the first thing he saw when he peered out of his shell hole at daybreak was a headless torso hugging a rifle.

During the worst fighting, a Marine acquaintance was blown to bits a few yards away, the blood and shredded flesh striking my father. "There was a roaring flash. He turned into a bloody mist. Nothing left of him. I tasted something funny while I dove for cover, and I realized it was that poor guy's blood on my mouth." Another shell sheared off most of a man's head but he ran for a few steps before he collapsed. Countless other men lost smaller pieces of themselves. Some were lucky enough to get a "good wound," the kind that wasn't life threatening but earned the sufferer a ticket home.

I tried to picture that revolting "bloody mist," amazed to hear my dad calmly describing all the gore he'd seen. It was Mom, the farmers' daughter, after all, who dispatched yucky bugs, docked puppies' tails, put cat-mauled birds out of their misery, extracted splinters or the sewing needle I once stepped on, and generally handled the trivial grossness of daily living. Dad was too squeamish and sensitive. Yet he talked without flinching about the weeping of dying men, their calls for their mothers. He was matter-of-fact about the men who broke down bawling or became empty-eyed zombies from too much time in combat. "Some of them were huge husky guys, college athletes. There was no telling who might crack up." More than one man he knew, including a big blowhard who'd pictured himself the ideal Marine and his company's much-loathed first sergeant, a.k.a. "Porky Pig," came unglued in the foxholes at night.

Dad admitted to his own nagging fears: that a bayonet or sword would come slashing at him when he was too tired and slow to protect himself, or the Japanese soldiers seen massing on the reverse slope would launch a banzai charge. He also imagined himself wounded and dragged by the enemy into one of the caves, to be tortured.

Finally, on May 19, the much-depleted Twenty-ninth Regiment secured Sugar Loaf and the Japanese swiftly evacuated further south. When Dad stumbled off the hill for good it was coated with smoking military debris, disabled and exploded tanks, and an indescribable array of body parts to be collected for burial. Bloated flies were already swarming. It was almost impossible to avoid stepping on the remains.

After Sugar Loaf my father was a grizzled Marine, the boot-camp idealist bumped off for good. "I was an unshaven, filthy, flea-bitten, mosquito-chawed stinking mess and my hand shook when I tried to light a cigarette. My skin was yellow from atabrine. I'm sure we all looked like wild men." His mouth curled. "And I had lice. Pretty gross, huh?" He survived Sugar Loaf with nothing worse than bruising, a wrenched ankle, infected feet and calves, and a few deep cuts. But before he'd even enjoyed his reward for living—a shave, bath, and hot meal—Dad was already brooding over why he was selected for survival. How in hell had he gotten out in one piece when so many others, "much better men," had not?

Although he'd done his duty, Dad felt undeserving of his safe passage through one of the war's nastiest fights. He had followed orders, aimed and fired his M-1, but in such furor it was impossible to know the outcome. Had he made up for his failure to shoot that Japanese soldier? He couldn't say. When he enlisted in the Marines he had daydreamed about demonstrating courage alongside his comrades. Instead, he came out of combat feeling like a lonely coward. In the aftermath of Sugar Loaf my father was sound on the outside but sick at heart.

CHAPTER NINE

DAD'S
WAR MOVIE

Jerry Collins with John Terrence (left) and Sy Ivice (center) in front of the mess tent on Guadalcanal

The division has been in the lines for a long time now. There is still rough fighting ahead but the final blow can come almost any time. This has really been a grinder and hard on men. When we will finally set up to rest and prepare for the next operation I don't know.... Tell little John Shirk that his communion really helped me because I had a close one, which blew my gear to shreds and killed a buddy. All those nice pictures you sent me no longer exist except as scattered fragments. The section was hit pretty hard and I've lost some good buddies.

(*Jerry Collins, on Okinawa, June 12, 1945*)

We few, we happy few, we band of brothers;
For he to-day that sheds his blood with me
Shall be my brother.

(*William Shakespeare*, Henry V)

In 1972 a tremendous fire destroyed St. Mary Church, toppling the bell tower, crushing the mighty columns, melting the gorgeous stained glass, and reducing Angy's queenly organ loft to blackened bits. In one night a longtime fixture of Collins family life was kaput. From then on Miff and I reluctantly accompanied Mom and Angy to the Catholic school auditorium, a drab stand-in till an architectural fiasco resembling a suburban bank branch took over the charred lot.

My father stopped going to mass altogether, abandoning all pretence at faith. When we left him behind each Sunday I pictured him moving freely about the house, relieved we were gone. I missed the sight of him in his spiffy hat and suit back when he still loomed over us all, smiling, self-contained, and assured. In the year since he'd moved back home I'd grown ashamed of my dad. At first I'd thrown myself at him, hoping he'd respond with that offhanded, easy affection I remembered from early childhood. Little by little I learned to hold back, to avoid the shock of his bewildered detachment. I'd thought he'd rebound from his disgrace, and act like a daddy again, but instead he drifted further into defeated isolation. Something inside him had shut down after the divorce. He fell out of sync, like a clock slowly losing time.

We all still depended on him, to fulfill his financial pact with Mom, help keep the Collins dinghy afloat, yet he failed relentlessly despite his Monday through Friday motions. Sensing trouble, Mom stepped up her pressure on him. It dismayed me that my mother, generous and good hearted with everybody else, spoke so harshly to my dad. "Other men manage to hold down a job, any job," she ranted. "If you can't make it in sales, Jerry Collins, then get a job at a gas station. Or bagging at the supermarket. Or flipping burgers at Jack's. Anything is better than a great big nothing!"

In response, he became more evasive about his work activities. Whenever he walked into the kitchen early in the afternoon, cutting short his sales calls long before the five o'clock whistle started shrieking over at the wire mill, he must have sensed how crestfallen I was. We were barely scraping by on Mom's tiny earnings, supplemented with her vast summer garden, ambitious canning-and-freezing operation, exhaustive coupon clipping, the slapdash sewing she taught Miff and me to save on school clothes, and other Depression-era thrift. She even put us to work manufacturing homemade cigarettes for her with a store-bought contraption, our dexterous fingers adept at rolling the papers and pumping the tobacco shred into them.

The visible evidence of our poverty made me increasingly self-conscious and I squarely blamed my ne'er-do-well dad. Soon adolescence became another wedge between us. The year St. Mary Church burned down I entered seventh grade in the aging fortress where my mom used to teach high school English. One morning she found a pair of spotted underpants in the wash and chased me down at the school to have a belated chat on womanhood. For quite some time I had wanted to ask her what my body was plotting, having heard upsetting descriptions. Unfortunately, menstruation had to do with sexual maturity, which had to do with having sex and making babies and being married—not a good topic to bring up with Mom. When my period arrived I pretended that it wasn't happening. Even after she rescued me, Mom could barely bring herself to discuss the bare facts.

Naturally, I had begun to ponder their blighted relationship. In marriage they'd slept together nightly and had five children. Then Dad strayed and had sex with other women. I'm not even certain Mrs. Ketchum was the last, because my sister later saw a photograph of a woman "friend" of his in a bathing suit, taken before the divorce was final. As for Mom, she never broke her wedding vows but after they split up she went out on a few dates before deciding: "That's it—no more men. I've had it up to here with them. I'm going to concentrate on my own life now." Now Mom and Dad occupied separate beds in the same house; their old passion buried away like toxic waste.

Menstruation, skin outbreaks, budding breasts, mood swings, thoughts of sex—the earthy elements of a girl's maturation made me all the more awkward around my keenly observant father. My unpopularity at school was a particular sore point, especially now that my little sister was beginning to shine socially. Moving from sixth to seventh grade I'd wound up separated from my friends again, and struggled to make new ones. Boys were becoming a factor in junior high success, and I was scared I'd be rejected. I could tell Dad was aware of what I was going through but he seemed incapable of expressing any direct concern or interest in me any more. Sometimes he made obnoxious gibes about my awkwardness or spotty appearance. His sense of humor, once so quick and witty, had gone off kilter and grown annoying, almost cruel. I shrank away from him, too upset and exposed to cope. Soon we were in danger of a mute coexistence, since neither of us could think of one safe thing to say.

Old movies came to our rescue. World War II movies made in the forties, fifties, and early sixties were frequent TV fare, and Dad and I—two loners with time on our hands—got into the habit of watching them together.

My father had always adored movies. As a teenager in the 1930s he was an usher at the Branford Theatre—a lucky break. To see the latest Hollywood offerings over and over again for free was an enviable perk during the Depression. It didn't matter what the film was—horse opera, romance, melodrama, mystery—he loved them all. During the war, from one training camp to the next, he made sure to attend every screening for the enlisted men, reporting his picks and pans to the folks back home. Then came the landing on Okinawa, and silver-screen fantasies were put on hold for a while. After the war the claustrophobia he'd developed living in close quarters in barracks, tents, and on troopships gradually put a stop to his movie going. The only film I ever watched with my dad was *Doctor Doolittle*, and he spent a good part it standing at the back of the theater near the exit. By then I'd noted how he liked to keep a nice thick cushion of empty air around him at all times. Later on, when I was old enough to attend Saturday matinees alone, I dutifully reported to the exiled film buff on the plots and players in *Tora! Tora! Tora!*, *Bridge on the River Kwai*, and other World War II fare.

Viewed on our little black-and-white set at 101 PO, in a small room just off the kitchen, Dad's favorite genre fostered an easy companionship between us requiring few words. He seemed pleased that I was there, taking an interest. We watched dozens of blood-and-guts flicks together, including *Pride of the Marines, Edge of Darkness, Thirty Seconds over Tokyo, Destination Tokyo, Assignment to Brittany, Guns of*

Navarone, Gung Ho!, For Whom the Bell Tolls, A Walk in the Sun, Twelve O'Clock High, From Here to Eternity, Wing and a Prayer.

Although the Army and Air Force hogged most of the screen time Dad set aside his old hard feelings for the sake of reconnecting to a vital part of himself. It didn't matter all that much if the TV drama centered on D-Day in France, or England during the Blitz, or Pearl Harbor, and never gave my father's invasion its turn in the spotlight. The passing decades had made him hungry for an entire era now extinct.

Even when the leading man wore an Army "doggie" helmet Dad could relate to the character's attitude and mindset, his way of talking. He did have strong preferences when it came to the actors, though. He detested John Wayne, with his overblown macho hero-ism. Dana Andrews was too wishy-washy. Errol Flynn didn't "ring true" as a fighting man. Gregory Peck, John Garfield, and Gary Cooper were all swell, however. Dad preferred the complicated, darker hero types to the swaggerers. He joked that Hollywood would have come clamoring for Jerry Collins "if they'd only caught my big screen test," that scrap of newsreel shot on Sugar Loaf Hill while he was racing forward to set up communications under fire.

It surprised me that Dad was so hot on the sentimental con-coctions Hollywood had cooked up from his war, with their blatant themes of blood brotherhood, selfless patriotism, personal redemp-tion through the ultimate sacrifice, and other popcorn pathos. Eventually I understood that even as the cornball excess elicited his cynical gibes, it rekindled the innocent idealism he'd started out with on Parris Island in 1943. As we relived his war in the movies I sensed in my father the unresolved conflict between that patriotic wide-eyed youth and the broken-spirited combat vet I knew. By the time the credits rolled Hollywood's visions of war had raised Dad high, then dumped him back into depression. Once the TV was turned off he got right up and left, to smoke away his sadness alone.

The war movies bugged Mom. She sometimes made dismissive comments or tried to get us to change the channel. I liked defying her on this, knowing Dad wouldn't defend himself. My mother's supremacy in our household was unquestionable, and sticking up for Dad's movies was nearly all I could or would do for him. "Come on, Ma," I protested. "You can't make us switch right in the middle. It's getting good." She gave me a pissy look but relented. And I really did enjoy the movies, despite their dated style and dialogue. I knew they left out the ugly realities, and sewed up plot lines all nice and neat, but the primary-colored emotions of the characters were compelling.

Dad invariably criticized the way filmmakers portrayed combat. "You'd be dead in an instant if you pulled that stunt, exposing yourself that way," he'd snort, disgusted by some character's foolhardy display of bravery. "They never show people killed by friendly fire, by their own side," he'd remark. "That happened quite a bit." Or, "look at that guy. Nobody handles a weapon like that." And still he watched, avidly.

"They should have consulted you," I said one time. "Or men like you, who were there."

"Nope." He shook his head. "Then they couldn't have made the movie at all. Nobody would want to see what really went on."

When a tough soldier cracked up in a film, Dad recalled a similar guy he'd known who did the same. When some kid was hit, bleeding to death in the arms of a buddy, with enough time to make poignant remarks, Dad snorted over the impossibly leisurely farewell but I could tell he was touched. He sat frowning at the jumpy screen making its ominous fizzing sounds, his chin trembling through the sad parts, his fingers gripping the arms of his captain's chair. Sometimes I found myself watching Dad more than the movie, wondering what thought made his face twist suddenly. I felt his surge of frustration when the terrible reception of our unreliable TV wiped out some key dialogue or scene and he frantically adjusted various knobs trying to get it back. It seemed as though what happened on that fickle screen mattered more than his real life.

Dad liked best the movies that focused on the camaraderie forged among fighting men. There was a tried-and-true formula bringing together a motley assortment of types—the tough-talking New Yorker, the drawling rural hayseed, the streetwise dropout, the college boy, the sensitive soul, the cocky athlete, the coward, the natural leader, and so forth. These men, unlikely friends in ordinary life, all bonded in combat and met their disparate fates under fire. These men, more or less, were Dad and his long-lost brothers from his old intelligence outfit.

The films we watched reminded Dad of more realistic, down-to-earth scenes from the war movie starring him and his buddies. There were quiet, nostalgic moments as the homesick boys talked through the night in the jungle heat, about the families they left behind, their postponed futures, and the fighting soon to come. Somber shots of exhausted men coming off the front line, staggering through the mud, each face coated with dirt and aged by the sight of too much killing. Huddled in a cave together, to escape the rain, and watching, awestruck and anxious, as swarms of kamikaze zeroed in on the Allied fleet in the harbor below, the explosions and anti-aircraft guns surpassing any imaginable fireworks extravaganza. Pulling pranks to lift each other's spirits. Offering wordless comfort on the loss of another comrade.

Eventually I figured out why the buddy flicks meant so much to Dad. No friendship after the war could compare to the intimacy he had known with his Marine comrades. In fact, he didn't have any postwar friendships to speak of, until close to the end of his life. When he was a young husband and father, just starting out in the working world, Dad still sought to connect with others. But I don't think his family—his parents, wife, or any of his kids—ever saw the Jerry Collins his fellow Marines had known and depended on wholeheartedly. That sense of solidarity and loyalty, no matter what, disappeared from his life after 1946.

Flawed as they were, inaccurate and soppy, those TV war movies recaptured Dad's intense wartime friendships, and the terrible, unpredictable loss that accompanied them. One of the hardest losses to bear was John Terrence, a big-hearted, larger-than-life figure beloved by all in Dad's unit.

He met John early in his tour of duty, at Camp Ritchie in Maryland. They bonded quickly—two Marines stuck in an Army camp, where they were undergoing intelligence training. Both were quick witted, sensitive, and kind. Tall and gangly, both excelled on the basketball court. But whereas Dad was a quiet observer, "Big John" was an irrepressible daredevil who enjoyed provoking senior officers and pulling off outrageous escapades. My father admired John, and enjoyed how he blithely thumbed his nose at authority. "He was an operator," he said, the highest possible praise. While all the men in Dad's outfit liked to fancy themselves operators, meaning they were constantly "borrowing" items that weren't nailed down, like food and clothing and gear, it was really John who excelled at the scrounging game. He also epitomized the Marine virtue of sharing. "Anything we got in the mail from home, anything we begged, borrowed, or stole got passed around," Dad said.

It was a sore point with many Marines that the Army always got the best food, weapons, and clothing, while they got whatever "crap" was left behind. Shortly after Sugar Loaf, with their intelligence outfit resting in reserve, John persuaded his close pal Sy Ivice to help him swipe an Army jeep. Then they rode off to a supply station where they passed themselves off as Army and finagled a box of combat boots. En route back to Marine territory, the pair persuaded some friendly "Seabees," a navy construction unit, to paint the Army jeep Marine green with fake ID numbers. Thanks to John and Sy's derring-do, Col. Robb, head of their battalion, got a new jeep while Dad and the rest of the men swapped their leaky boon-dockers for superior Army footwear.

The unit sorely needed this morale boost. All of the men were worn down from combat, flea-bitten and filthy from days of slog-ging in mud up to their thighs. Despite the enemy's defeat at Sugar Loaf Hill, battles continued to rip apart the island. The Japanese were fighting to the last man, even as malnutrition and illness began crippling their dwindling forces. They blasted the Americans with kamikaze assaults, heavy artillery, machine gun fire, and massive shells, including a new breed of low-velocity rocket mortars launched from rails, notoriously inaccurate, which were dubbed "screaming meemies" for their piercing shrieks.

Days after John and Sy's big heist, the Second Battalion, Twenty-ninth Regiment took part in the last Marine amphibious assault of World War II, landing on the Oroku peninsula in prepa-ration for a final push on to Naha and the southernmost tip of the island. That night John, my father, and the rest of their outfit sought shelter from a hard rain in a cemetery populated with the traditional family tombs where Okinawans venerated the ashes of their ancestors. The men far preferred bivouacking in the tombs to sleeping in soggy foxholes exposed to the rotten weather and enemy fire. "We all sacked out in one tomb," Dad told me. "I was exhausted and conked right out."

Around dawn the men began to rise, to set out on their patrol duties. Dad was struggling to wake up when he heard a screaming meemie in the distance. "An ungodly, high-pitched shriek. I won-dered 'Where's it gonna hit?' And then I knew. Right on top of us."

That was his last thought before he was knocked uncon-scious. When he came to, the tomb was filled with smoke and debris and an overpowering chemical stink. Another man stumbled over my father who lay there stunned, his hearing dulled from the blast. "I'm okay," he thought, but he couldn't move. He tried to call out to the others, to see how they were doing, but he couldn't summon his voice.

Then he heard somebody say, "John's hit bad."

The screaming meemie had struck just outside the tomb entrance, in the walled courtyard where John had been heating a cup of instant coffee. "Half of John's leg was blown off," Dad said, his eyes flooding. "I heard him calling for a priest. He died on the way to the hospital. My gear was blown to smithereens. My nerves were shot to hell. But I walked away with a few bumps and bruises, that's all."

My father lost many comrades on Okinawa, some in ways he could not bear to describe in more than a few words. The death of John Terrence especially haunted him, however, and he recounted it numerous times. "It knocked the stuffing out of all of us," he told me. "It was tough to keep on going." In addition to losing John, the unit suffered other casualties in the attack, sending a couple of men home with serious injuries, and was never again the same tightly knit band.

After Dad died I found some photos of John in his suitcase of mementos—of the two of them with Sy Ivice on Guadalcanal, cleaning their mess kits outside the mess tent, and the famous contest in which the same three flaunted their noses to determine whose was biggest. John was also in my father's favorite picture, the one all soft and blurred from frequent handling, of their outfit posing in the jungle.

Eventually I got in touch with Dad's surviving comrades, three of whom shared their memories of the day the screaming meemie hit. William Manchester described the blast, which wounded him severely, when I paid a visit to his house. It is also in his war memoir *Goodbye, Darkness*. Tim Joyner wrote about it in the *Marine Family Newsletter*. He was off on assignment when John died, but heard the screaming meemie careering toward its target and returned to find "our little section decimated."

And finally, Sy Ivice, John's partner in the jeep-and-boots heist, wrote to me about his dear friend's death. He sent me an account of the attack on the tomb recorded by the "other" Jerry in the unit, Jeremiah O'Neill, now deceased. Evacuated for medical care, fledgling author Bill Manchester left behind his Okinawa journal, which O'Neill found and carried on. While some small details are incorrect, understandable under duress, it could as easily have been Jerry Collins writing about the day John died:

> Am continuing this where Bill left off. At 0830 about 12 of us all crowded in a tomb as the Japs have been throwing [spigot] [m]ortars at us. They are about 12 feet long and 500 pounds. John Terrence was out in the yard...getting some chow. Bill, Jerry C., Nick, [Frank], Sy and I were in the tomb. Then a sudden explosion. The tomb rocked and filled with [black picric] acid gas. Shrapnel flew and when I came to, my whole body was wracked from concussion; John was lying across the tomb door as I managed to crawl out, his left leg blown almost off up to the knee. I called for corpsmen. When Dr. got there I was holding John's head in my lap and he kept asking for a priest...the Dr. kept telling him he wasn't going to die. I had to lead Sy out the black smokey [sic] hole as he was severely cut over the eyes and could not see. He kept saying as I led him out, "Watch out Ace, I don't want to step on John." Jerry C. was only shocked, likewise Nick. Bill was wounded on left side and badly shocked. Bill, [Frank], and Sy were evacuated. My nerves are shot. If the Lord sees fit...I can hold out until the operation is over—we now have 8 men left out of 16....

> (June 5, 1945)

So there it was again, that familiar scene from Dad's war movie, capturing forever John Terrence's heartbreaking fate. It would have done my father good to know his old buddies never got over that day either—too mundane, horrific, and full of pointless loss for any Hollywood production.

CHAPTER TEN

COMBAT FATIGUE

Young Jerry Collins at the beach in Branford

After 82 days of fighting the battle of Okinawa has been won. In these brief and terse words Admiral Chester W. Nimitz announced to a waiting world that American ships, planes, tanks, and men had written a chapter of glorious victory on the very doorstep of Japan.... However, there can be little of elation over this triumph, costliest of all campaigns in the Central and Western Pacific fighting.... This victory on Okinawa should serve as a stern reminder of the task which yet lies ahead. The price which the Japanese paid, some 90,400 killed and 4,000 taken prisoner in futile defense of this strip of land so vital to their welfare, should give emphasis to the fanatical resistance which may be expected when the final blows are mounted on the Jap homeland or upon its holdings in China.

(New Haven Evening Register,
Friday, June 22, 1945, clipped by Jerry's parents)

I suppose you can consider the island secured now. We went south after my last letter and rolled down to the beach. Now we are mopping up, which is quite a task as the Nips dig in and hide like animals rather than surrender. Whatever makes you figure I'll be home by Thanksgiving? Had it not been for the Marines there would be another two months of fighting here. Someone has to serve as shock troops ... only they use us over and over again. You can take the Army in the Pacific and do with them as you wish. I know what I'd like to do. As long as the Japs hold out the Marines will be making beachheads....

(Jerry to his parents, June 23, 1945)

During the months Jerry was in combat on Okinawa, his hero FDR died and Germany surrendered. He took little note, however, for his war still ran scorching hot. The surging battles and constant stress engulfed him until well into June, when the Japanese Army finally collapsed and its leaders committed *seppuku*, or ritual suicide. Later Jerry would write home: "When we were in combat our section was the outfit in our company that stuck its neck out, and though we were the smallest unit we had the most killed. Everyone steered clear of us then because they knew that wherever we were the bullets and shells were also."

Most of the deaths he'd witnessed were random: a sniper's bullet found one fellow when he paused to adjust his pack, another died playing cards, and John Terrence was hit while brewing coffee. A week after the screaming meemie killed John one more pointless death overwhelmed the weary outfit. One of its young pups, Nick Praxitalas, made a thoughtless, impulsive move. While out scouting Japanese defenses "Prax" spotted a pile of Japanese rifles abandoned outside a cave. Enticed by the chance to nab a prized souvenir he grabbed hold, pulled, and the booby-trapped weapons blew up, killing him instantly. He was the last of Jerry's close buddies to die on Okinawa, a bitter finale.

In the final weeks of June, after fighting on the Oroku peninsula and Kuwanga Ridge, Jerry's regiment took part in mop-up operations to flush out the last of the defeated enemy. One of his ghoulish tasks was to search the dead for ID, his stomach churning with self-loathing as he rummaged among the rotting bodies. Sometimes he watched while Marine flamethrowers torched caves where the enemy had holed up, refusing to surrender. Many Okinawans were trapped among them. As the conflict ground on, Jerry had witnessed the burning of homes and villages, the bombing by both sides of the Okinawans' sacred tombs. He saw the burnt and mangled remains of the helpless islanders, many children among them. He felt no pity or remorse, however. The out-of-body sensations he'd experienced on Sugar Loaf hung on. He performed his duties with dull-witted diligence, an icy "just doing my job" attitude that distanced him from the trauma all around. It was hard to mourn others when he couldn't summon up concern for himself. Sure, he'd made it this far, but the mammoth invasion of Japan lay ahead.

As fresh replacements arrived it began to sink in how many familiar faces were gone for good. Jerry and his fellow combat veterans shared their stories of close calls and death scenes. Letters from home brought news of more Branford boys killed in other countries. Only dreams of the future kept Jerry from brooding: "Oh those coming days at Yale! I plan and re-plan them every day. They seem in the dim future but I know they are coming and I can wait...."

At last the bullets stopped flying and the island fell quiet. On July 2, 1945, the invasion of Okinawa was officially over. The commanding generals on both sides were dead. The death toll was approximately 23,000 Americans, 93,000 Japanese, and 150,000 Okinawans—more than the losses of Nagasaki and Hiroshima combined. Fourteen percent of all US Marines killed in World War II died on this island. Jerry's division suffered the greatest losses: 1,656 dead, 7,429 wounded, and 11 missing; and his regiment, the Twenty-ninth, suffered the most deaths: 551.

The resilience of youth, so vital to waging war, had been fully exploited on Okinawa. While he waited to shove off for Guam, where the Marines were to rest and regroup, Jerry struggled with combat fatigue and a new sense of futility.

"I'll lay odds I'll live through another war," he wrote his parents, scoffing at the historic meeting in San Francisco where representatives of fifty countries signed the UN Charter. "The greater nations all spout world organizations and peace but none will sacrifice a damn thing to get it. All I can see coming out of this conference is a lot of compromises and millions of 'ifs' and 'buts.' I know

I'm not fighting any war to end all wars. Only an egghead would believe that. I'm fighting for democracy but mainly to get home."

In the aftermath of Okinawa, sickened by the meat-grinder reality of combat, Jerry sounded less and less like a proud Marine and more and more like the disillusioned man who was my dad.

* * *

Happy are the men who yet before they are killed
Can let their veins run cold...
And some cease feeling
Even themselves for themselves.
Dullness best solves
The tease and doubt of shelling.

(Wilfred Owen, WWI poet, "Insensibility")

In the early seventies, as the Vietnam War rushed to its brutal end, Dad's war came to seem even to me a remote affair and his nostalgia for it a disturbing weakness. We gradually stopped watching our World War II movies. Our conversations became short and shallow. We occupied the same house, ate at the same table. We shared the same narrow face and brown eyes, so dark the pupils appear to have melted into melancholy pools. But whereas Dad was fleeing inside himself, shedding his substance, I was clawing my way into focus, an emergent teenager acutely aware of my every atom, craving recognition and attention.

Despite our growing separation, I couldn't retract my antennae where Dad was concerned. I could tell he was starting to give up. He devoted dwindling hours to tooling about Connecticut byways on hapless sales missions and was spending a greater part of Monday through Friday in his room, pretending to organize his accounts and posting affirmations he'd written on file cards. "$50,000 this year!" said one. "Double this month's target!" urged another. When my mother picked up on his "slacking off," a new cycle of rage and frustration commenced. "You have some nerve, Jerry Collins," was her refrain. "I work twice the hours you do. I'm the only one keeping things together here."

During this period I read Arthur Miller's *Death of a Salesman* for my eighth-grade literature class. It struck me that Dad and Willy Loman had a lot in common—two casualties in the pursuit of the American Dream. My father wasn't the bullying braggart Willy was but they both clung desperately to their outdated aspirations, destroying their families in the process.

Late one night that summer, my grandmother died abruptly of a heart attack after returning from one of her social whirls. I woke in deep darkness to the sounds of urgent voices in her room downstairs as a strange vehicle crunched up the gravel driveway, lights flashing. I didn't understand till morning what had transpired. By then my grandmother's bed was empty, and Dan the dachshund had managed to hoist his fat sausage trunk onto the naked mattress to pine in a patch of sunlight, his life force slipping off to join hers. Compared to that grumpy old dog, my dad showed little emotion over Angy's passing.

In her will, Angy left the homestead to all nine of her Collins and Sadowski grandchildren, along with small bequests. Everything else went to her daughter Alice, except for a modest sum for her disappointing son. My father stood poker-faced as the lawyer droned from one legalism to the next. Dad had run through plenty of Angy's money but it was still a crushing blow to discover how little was left of the former Collins land-based wealth. The amount set aside for him immediately went toward his debts. Angy's will barely acknowledged my mother, an inexplicable cold-shouldering she never got over. My brothers took on the awkward duty of negotiating to buy out our cousins' shares of 101 PO so Mom and Miff and I—and silent, tight-lipped Dad—wouldn't be left homeless.

The new mortgage slapped onto the house terrified Mom. How could she pay it? Then, miraculously, she scored a secretarial position at Yale, Dad's alma mater, and our years of unpredictable hand-to-mouth finances were over. The economic power at 101 PO shifted decisively and permanently from Dad to Mom. While the Yale job was a sympathy hire, one older woman giving another a break, it didn't take long for Mom to prove herself indispensable. "If I were only younger," she took to musing, "I could see myself becoming a career woman."

Just as her fortunes improved, however, Dad's commissions petered out again. His car was repossessed for nonpayment, and to make his sales calls he had to borrow the used clunker Mom had purchased. She didn't make that easy. "I didn't buy my car for your personal use, Jerry Collins," she huffed. "You better believe I'm going to add wear and tear and insurance costs to the money you already owe me."

The IRS set after Dad for unpaid back taxes. The government's fruitless quest would continue until he was in his grave, as one implacable agent after another hounded my father into a state of agitated wretchedness. "Taxes? On what," my mother said scornfully, ignoring his distress. "You tell them, Jerry, how you haven't paid me a dime for child support or alimony in months. You tell them how your children have gone without basic needs because you can't keep a job!" Once I heard her badgering him to tell the agent he was a World War II vet whose psychological impairments made him unable to keep a steady job. That was the only occasion in Dad's lifetime that I ever heard her mention the effects of his war, and it offended him into an angry outburst. "Shut up about that, Blanche!" he bellowed, with rare spirit, storming about the kitchen. "Not another word! I'll work something out with the IRS but I'm not saying any bullshit like that!" He stalked out of the house. When he returned some time later he had reverted to his subdued self.

To escape the acrimony he began to revisit his cloudless childhood, the unsullied joys of growing up in Branford. My sister and I stifled our impatience as he retold goofy anecdotes we'd already heard countless times. He rarely joked anymore, except with Jennifer, and his old swagger was gone. He moved quietly about the house and yard, performing his chores at the pace of a much older man. He hand washed and hung out all his own clothing, refusing to use Mom's washer and dryer. I loathed the sight of his worn undershirts and boxer shorts, and spent money I made babysitting on new ones, which I sneaked onto the clothesline a few at a time, interspersing the snowy white among the fraying dull grey, hoping he wouldn't notice and feel humiliated. When he set off for work I observed that his ties were thin when they should be fat. His suits had fallen years out of fashion but a new one was out of the question. Mom never would have cottoned to diverting household funds so my dad could properly "dress for success."

I was old enough to understand that most of her lashing fury came from old hurt over Dad's dalliance with Mrs. Ketchum; and second to that, her terror of poverty. But despite her bitter words she sometimes acted peculiarly loyal to him, if in a begrudging, spotty fashion. She would prepare roast beef or chicken 'n' dumplings, his favorites, and the parsnips only he liked. If she noticed holey socks of his hanging on the clothesline she took them in to darn. She silently repaired broken zippers and replaced missing buttons on his shirts. When he got sick with one of his frequent respiratory ailments, she made sure he had Vick's Vapo-Rub and cough syrup. She bought him a thickly lined corduroy jacket at a yard sale, and while the hand-me-down hurt his pride he immediately retired his threadbare trench coat to wear it instead. It struck me that Mom hadn't entirely shucked the role of Mrs. Jeremiah F. Collins after all. She might claim to want to turn back the clock and become a career woman, but she still longed to be a wife too.

The year I became a freshman my brother Peter finally took off for the University of Connecticut. He'd already stuck around an extra year, deferring college in order to make money and help Mom. I wasn't sure how we would get by without him. With my brothers all gone and Angy dead, it was just my sister and me and Mom and Dad now, in a house that seemed distressingly melancholy.

My sister rebelled sometimes, infuriated by our parents' inability to act more like her friends' moms and dads, but I caused no concern. I was the sort of teenaged girl that adults automatically trusted: sensible, self-contained, and apparently content, never giving cause for alarm. I struggled to be polite to my father and to help Mom out around the house. Outwardly I was emulating my brothers' merit-badge behavior, but inside I was eager to revolt.

Disconnected at home, I felt equally at a loss at the high school my three brothers had also attended. A number of teachers were still praising their virtues, which made me wonder where my own talents lay. On my heels, my sister was flourishing at the middle school, acting in plays, singing in talent shows, attracting friends with her natural charm. I began to think I was a lot like my Dad, doomed to stand apart, watching others lead the full life I desired.

One day my expository writing teacher instructed the class to write an essay continuing from this opening statement: "I am good for something." When he read my hedging, response Mr. Zimmerman took up where my fifth-grade teacher Mr. Grosh had left off, retorting in his distinctive script beneath an "A+" that I was underestimating myself. Deep down, I believed he was right. But whenever I went home, I lost faith. Seeing Dad mired in failure made me doubt my own worth. Looking about me at the cheerleaders and majorettes, the jocks and party animals, the student council leaders, actors, comedians, and eggheads, even the dorky band members, townie miscreants, and total losers, I couldn't see where I fit in. Really, Mr. Z, what exactly WAS I good for? I was desperate to find out.

Then I turned sixteen and a door suddenly opened: I got a job at the local Friendly's, which back then was a hot spot in my podunk town, the place everybody wound up after the movies, high school games, shopping excursions, bowling league tournaments, shifts at the local factories. My regulars included a homeless mentally ill couple who occupied counter seats for hours on end; a man who suffered from a form of leprosy; a friendly prostitute who enjoyed her work; a lonely single mother of six children; and a heroin addict who confided his daily teeter-tottering between using and abstaining. It was amazing how readily other people gave up their secrets to an amateur shrink in an apron dispensing distracted "mm-hmmms" and bottomless cups of coffee.

While providing an unexpected education, my job at that wholesome watering hole also threw me in with an older crowd. I was chummy with employees close to my own age, and I even had a crush on a high school junior from another town, but some impulse drew me to the hard-living types on the payroll who averaged a decade older than me. One or two were college graduates but most had no ambitions beyond the next paycheck. I liked their anything-goes attitude, the way they took it for granted that I had been around the block a few times myself.

Soon I was leading a secret life, pulling the wool over my parents' eyes with a depressing ease. I stayed out late on school nights, wildly guzzling Singapore slings, sombreros, and other training-wheel mixed drinks at the local gin mills with my new pals. I began hiding my nightgown outdoors, in a plastic shopping bag I stuck among some bushes away from the house. That way when I reeled home from the bars and parties at two and three and four AM I could change behind a tree and slip indoors. I had a pretext handy—I was letting in one of the cats—in case anyone saw me come in. A part of me knew full well that I was following in my father's footsteps, finding excitement and identity in stealthy nighttime activity, in booze and entanglements with guys I would never bring home.

I wasn't a loose girl, but I must have projected the aura of one because I swiftly went from wallflower to coveted counter girl—despite the hairnet and grey pilgrim uniform with white nursey shoes. My first six months on the job I had a couple of shift supervisors interested me, one of whom was already engaged. Another man, newly divorced and a father, asked me out. An air traffic controller also pursued me, and he was so thoughtful and good looking that I came dangerously close to having sex with him in his car, Rod Stewart caterwauling "Tonight's the Night" on the radio, when I suddenly thought to ask if he was married.

"Uh, well, yes," he stammered. "Though not like you'd think."

"Oh!" I pushed his hands away and snapped my seat back into its upright position. I took myself pretty lightly but I was not a dolt. "I'm no floozy," I snapped. "I'm only in high school! You'd better take me back," thinking as I gave my orders that I was quite the woman of the world. "We're through."

He continued to lie in wait for me after my shifts, pleading for another chance. One evening I was heading to Mom's car, the air traffic controller dogging behind, when another suspicion popped into my head. "Do you have any kids?"

Yes, he admitted, a son.

It had seemed like a game, acting in control, leading him on a chase, but at that moment I knew the truth: I was a naive teenager emanating need and longing, ripe for duping by older guys on the make. At least this one had told the truth when asked. I told him to go home and be with his family. "Don't come by to see me ever again," I snapped, as I climbed in the car and slammed the door.

As he slunk off I felt relieved but scared. What if I'd gotten involved with him and then found out about his family? I would have been the Other Woman, Ms. Ketchum, at age sixteen! My mother and father were too wrapped up in their problems, exhausted from the strain of living together, to sense how precipitously I'd become an adult, with sex all at once a casual, everyday option. They apparently gave no thought to the prospect of me dating or messing around. I'd gotten no advice from them, ever, about how to look after myself when it came to boys, or what standards of behavior to expect and demand. In the romantic marketplace I had no idea what value to place on myself. It was up to me to figure it all out. I determined to be very careful, to hold myself dear. But I also called Planned Parenthood that week and made an appointment for a diaphragm fitting because for all my sensible caution part of me was eager to throw myself into the ring, take my chances. I thought I couldn't do worse than Mom and Dad.

That's how a few months later I wound up on an East Haven beach after midnight, on a July night, drinking red wine with a man I hardly knew, a smooth-talking part-owner of a new restaurant and my oldest date yet. I was floating in reckless inebriation, chortling like a ninny because I realized I'd gotten myself into a sticky-wicket this time—picnicking by moonlight on a deserted unfamiliar strand ten miles from home with an almost-stranger who I didn't even like much. He'd looked better to me when a coworker introduced us. In the course of our date I noted with growing distaste the fussy haircut, ironed blue jeans, over-bright eyes, and prowling hands. I suspect he thought his owning a steak house was a powerful aphrodisiac to a small-town nobody like me.

I chugged my *vino* and pondered: if I dumped him on the spot would he bring me home? He reached out to touch my lips with his fingertips. Then all at once he rolled on top of me, flattening my lungs, dive-bombing my face with wet kisses, his hands staking claim in six places at once, fumbling with my skirt and underpants.

"No, don't," I said. "Get off me." He shut me up with his mouth. For a minute my brain left the scene, to stand off and watch, disdainful and strangely disconnected. Now you're in a fix, Julie. What did you expect? Taking risks, going off with a man you hardly know.

I heard the jingle of his belt buckle coming undone and my head instantly cleared. I thought of the Army knife. We'd used it to slice the fancy cheese he'd brought along. It was lying close by. I reached out a hand and the knife was right there, ready and willing.

"Stop it," I said, testing. "Hey!" I said his name loudly.

He grunted into my chest as he slid his blue jeans partway over his buttocks.

"Hey!"

God, he weighed a ton. His big arms were busy on me. The sand scraped my bare ass as he nudged himself inside.

"Get off me!"

"Baby, baby, please takeiteasy isso good—" His mashed-potato mumbling and clumsiness were the last straw. Enraged, I grabbed the knife and drove it into him, through a thick layer of denim.

I suppose that was a date rape, and that I answered one assault with another. He yelped when the knife went in but it didn't hurt him much, really. After all, it was a little knife and I didn't mean to inflict serious damage. I gave him a short bloody gash, not very deep because of the denim protecting his upper thigh. He pulled off his pants and I held them for him while he ran into the ocean to splash salt water on the wound. I washed the knife with some wine and snapped it shut, thinking, for one weird instant, of my dad.

Then I got an earful about my violent behavior. But my date wasn't a bad guy and my tender age suddenly made him extremely nervous, so in the end he did what he termed "the gentlemanly thing" and transported me back to Branford, depositing me a few blocks from my house at my request. It was around two AM, and I was completely sober. He roared off in his English convertible and I walked the rest of the way home, reviewing the episode with out-of-body detachment, contemplating what my beleaguered parents would do if I informed them that a man had forced himself on me, that I stuck him with a knife. I doubted they could handle it. It was their role to shake things up—mine was to be unobtrusive, lie low, and cause no concern. I knew I would say nothing, in the end, for fear of their weary responses—Mom's guilty panic mingled with Catholic reproach, Dad's predictable retreat. Besides, I liked my secret life, even after what had happened, and was not about to let either of them in on it.

I slipped on my nightgown and stowed my clothing as usual in the backyard bushes. When I walked into the kitchen all the lights were out. A sudden shift in the dark gave me an awful jolt. Mom, lying in wait? No, it was my father, standing by the stove and smoking. "Oh, Dad, you startled me," I said, hoping he wasn't close enough to smell wine on my breath.

"Hi, Chule. Where ya been?"

"I thought I heard one of the cats fighting outside so I came downstairs to check."

"Mmm hmmmm." He inhaled thoughtfully. "That's interesting. I've been standing right here, for at least an hour."

My thoughts flapped around wildly, like a bird trapped inside a room. What a dunce I was. I'd thought I was so slick and sly. Those nights I crept in late my sleepless father was probably listening from the other room or his bed upstairs. Now that he'd become almost invisible it was easy to overlook him and forget how sharply observant he was.

"Oh, I went out the sun porch door. The fight was on the front lawn." That was a bad, blatant lie. We rarely used that door and it was swollen shut in the heat, almost impossible to open. "I'm going to sleep now, Dad." I darted toward him, pecked his cheek, and sped toward the stairs.

"You be careful, Julie," I heard him mutter from the kitchen.

I paused for a second, hoping he might call after me, demand I tell him the truth, interrogate me a little. "Where are you coming in from, Julie? And who were you with?" He didn't, of course. I stumbled on a stair, shot through with sadness. He was my father, after all. Yet I couldn't remember a time he'd stepped in to tell me what's what, or to keep me safe. Even now, regardless of whatever he knew or guessed he only hung back, as usual, leaving me to go my own way, choose my own weapon.

CHAPTER ELEVEN COLD WAR

6-6 SOUTHERN TIP OF OKINAWA

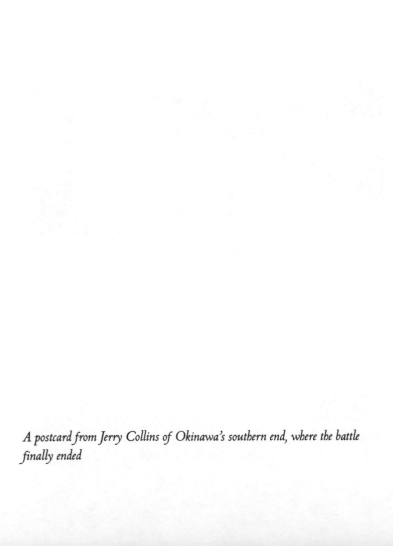

A postcard from Jerry Collins of Okinawa's southern end, where the battle finally ended

The news reports concerning atomic bombs and Russia [moving into Manchuria] and Japanese surrender had us gasping for breath. Nevertheless at last we can think to ourselves, no more fighting.... Yale and home seem so close today when a week ago they seemed a long way off. In our tent we are discussing what we'll do when we first get home and what sort of wardrobe of civilian clothes we will buy. I'll never regret being in the Marine Corps because it has taught me so much and is undoubtedly the greatest fighting outfit in the world. It was miraculous the way we fought through Okinawa without the excess equipment of the Army and how our division alone took about 4/5 of the island. It is something to brag about and all credit goes to the enlisted man who time and time again has to struggle through every form of fire to gain the objective. They win the wars and gain the least.... At last you can cease your worrying and one of these days the old salt will be heading home.

(August 16, 1945)

Jerry left Okinawa in the second week of July. His transport battled with a typhoon on the way to Guam, where the remains of his outfit rested and were given busywork, Marine-style. Jerry filled his free time slipping off to the PX, socializing with a group of Branford fellows, trying to study in the stultifying heat, and cadging beer between training exercises and work parties. "Managed to guzzle about an even dozen cold brews yesterday which helps to make life a little better," he wrote. So began the habit of drowning sadness with booze that I witnessed many times growing up.

When his parents raised the prospect of an imminent surrender Jerry was dubious. His war would last at least another year, he predicted, given Japan's "fight to the last man" code. Nonetheless, the quickening reports of peace feelers made even this jaded Marine start to hope. Then Churchill lost the election—"it was bad enough to lose Roosevelt at this time but now the Big Three is really broken up"—and he feared the peace talks would collapse.

Before he had the chance to write again, the United States dropped the first atom bomb on Hiroshima on August 6 and the second on Nagasaki three days later. "The big news here is the same as it is where you are," he wrote on August 12. "Everyone is talking about the atom bomb and especially about Japan's latest peace 'offer.' Naturally, we are practically standing on our hands waiting for it all to be acted upon."

The news of Japan's unconditional surrender on August 14 reached Guam as Jerry was heading out for a work party. He thought wistfully of the ticker tape parades that would take place back in the States. That same day more than two million people gathered in Times Square to celebrate V-J Day.

His war had come to a stunning end. However, as a single man with no dependents, Jerry knew he wouldn't see Branford any time soon. Stuck on another island indefinitely, his enthusiasm for Marine discipline worn thin by combat, he chafed at the petty humiliations that were the Leathernecks' common lot. His letters, though censored still, made his feelings clear. He wrote impatiently of "the great suppression of initiative and ambition of the enlisted men." And he looked forward to the reverses of civilian life, when privates would be hiring officers. "I'll stack the intelligence and ability of this section against any group in the battalion. They have been held back for a time but the new day isn't far around the corner."

On September 14, Jerry's twenty-third birthday passed without him even noticing. Finally, in October he bid the tropics farewell forever and shipped out for his tour of occupation duty in China, a country he'd been curious about ever since he'd read Pearl Buck novels and missionary accounts. In mid-October his battalion disembarked at the port city of Tsingtao and moved into a former school. "It isn't much like the old 2nd Battalion that landed on Okinawa, and not nearly as good," he noted. "The original outfit was certainly sharp but we are dull on the edges now."

Soon after his arrival, Jerry finally got a much belated reward, a bump up to corporal status. At first Cpl. Collins's letters rhapsodized on the sights and sounds of Tsingtao. He buzzed about in rickshaws, relaxed in the bathhouses, haggled in the markets over silk, wool, and jade ("I'm a big arm-waving, fist-shaking bargainer"), quaffed Chinese beer in cafes with imported monikers like Dreamland, Slim's, the Astor Roof, Blue Moon, and Golden Gate, and sampled rich cuisine in Russian restaurants. (In letters to friends, he also noted a rash of romances between Marine buddies and White Russian women.)

Within weeks, however, he had wearied of Marine drudgery and his new MP guard duties. The urban squalor of Tsingtao became oppressive to the small town native. "All about are beggars and hungry children," he wrote. "There is so much to be done that [Chiang] Kai-Shek must wonder if it is in the least possible. They haven't got unity yet, and that is a necessary step." Recommended for a sergeant's stripe, he decided to take the test even though a promotion "means about as much to me now as a refrigerator means to an Eskimo." His old determination to rise in rank had taken its last breath on Okinawa; his sole objective now was to go home.

In November he became an acting sergeant and got a cushy job teaching geometry and physics. He also trained new recruits to operate machine guns in imaginary combat, now that the real stuff was over. His letters, uncensored at last, questioned the Marines' vague mission in China and US meddling in the power struggle between the Chinese Nationalists and Communists. He resented how the enlisted men were shuttled about like chess pieces while the career military seemed hell-bent on flexing American muscle. With Japan soundly beaten there was nothing to safeguard in China, as far as Jerry could tell, so why keep men like him on the hook? "There may be a civil war here and I'm not sure how we'll stand," he wrote. "They've got us in an embarrassing position and getting us out of it will be a neat trick. The Communists rightfully don't want us here and of course the Nationalists have their own obvious reasons for wanting Marines on hand." His populist streak, deepened in combat, made him sympathetic to the Communists "who have every right on their side if they let a few loose in our direction because it seems obvious that we are taking sides."

Rumors flew that ships were coming into port to take Marines home, but one after another they skirted Tsingtao when the top brass insisted the men couldn't be spared. With Jerry and his peers noisily sounding off about their long stay in China, a colonel was appointed to hear the complaints. Cpl. Collins represented his section and recorded a bit of dialogue for his parents' amusement:

> Colonel, exactly what is our purpose in being here?
>
> Corporal, I'm not quite sure but I think the president wants us here.
>
> Why is it that we expect Russia to live up to her treaty [with China] when we are here against the published protests by both Chinese parties?
>
> I'm not up on the subject to give a good answer.

Jerry was also growing disillusioned with the incomplete peace that had been won with the lives of so many, including beloved buddies, and dubious about how long it would last. The Allies' wartime relationship was already cooling in these early, anxious days of the nuclear age. "Now stand by for a burst of fire," he wrote his parents in a long letter venting frustration. "Today's headline in the [Army newspaper] *Stars and Stripes* is 'US May Fight.' Makes a guy feel swell when we are supposedly through with war." He continued:

"The US could forge a complete peace but lots of people would have to give up their blood money investments. I'm burned and I've plenty more to say when I'm home. I may even run for selectman." He signed off, "All my love, Karl Marx."

In December, bitter weather arrived in Tsingtao. Jerry distracted himself with his teaching, playing basketball as one of the top scorers on the division's first-place team, and listening to stateside music and news on the radio. In his letters he mentioned recent shows of American might in China that had resulted in Marine plane crashes and loss of life. "I can't see this demonstration of power because the entire world by now knows our strength. The US is being quite aggressive...and has about as much diplomacy as Brownie," the Collins cocker spaniel.

Christmas came and went. At year's end Jerry heard disturbing scuttlebutt that Marines might be assigned to positions outside Tsingtao, to defend against the Communists. The Cold War was heating up. And my dad, marooned on its front edges, was in a prime position to note some of the first harbingers.

The morale of trigger-happy, battle-weary Marines in North China is lousy. From Tientsin to Chinwangtao, in garrisons, guarding railroad tracks, or repatriating Japs, more and more Leathernecks are cracking up daily.... [W]hen the Leathernecks started pouring into China in September and October, officers of many outfits frankly were afraid the Marines' rigid training and discipline would not be sufficient to check the tide of resentment that rose when the men became convinced they were merely pawns in a political chess game.... Not until the combat-worn, homesick veterans are home, replaced by low-pointers and regular Marines, will the moral of America's Leathernecks in China begin to climb toward normalcy....

(New Haven Evening Register, *November 1946*)

* * *

As I finished high school, Mom and Dad were fighting their own cold war. The hot disputes of the early postdivorce years—full of boozing, shouting, physical blows, furious door slamming—petered out and a different sort of conflict set in. My parents had adjusted to their uneasy cohabitation, but their simmering hostility made peace provisional, subject to unpredictable bursts of fire, usually when Mom, the superior power, felt Dad wasn't upholding his part of their bargain.

Now that I was earning money in my after-school and summer jobs, I felt a growing empathy for my mom. After all, she not only worked at an office job, leaving home earlier and returning later than Dad did, but also dedicated her free time to housework, gardening, and valiant attempts to make our deteriorating home attractive. Her gutsy grappling with daily life made his general detachment all the starker. He was caught in quicksand, sinking a bit more each year. But he didn't seem to care. He had stopped wanting anything for himself. And it wasn't for lack of materialism; it was for lack of self. Buying him a birthday or Christmas present was a hopeless task because his wish list was always blank. "Nuttin', Chule," he invariably said if I asked. "Save your money for yourself." My single inspiration, ever, was a subscription to *National Geographic*, which he devoured.

Mom on the other hand craved all sorts of things: a bentwood rocker, a real Coach handbag, a late frost, Shalimar perfume, a grandfather's clock, a bluebird sighting, a better car. She also gave prodigiously to others despite her small income. Every weekend young children came knocking for the treats she kept on hand for them. She stuffed bags with garden produce for the neighbors. She made meals and did errands for an elderly couple she'd befriended during a brief involvement with the local Socialist party.

Sometimes Mom would talk wistfully of the mysterious "companion" she wished for—someone to accompany her to concerts and the theater, to talk with her about books and poetry and music. I knew what she really wanted was the husband she had thought Dad would be. Even in the midst of their cold wrangling she reminisced about the years when they had parented together. "I wish you kids could have seen him with each of you, when you were babies," she mused. "Jerry was the most gentle, loving father, not like any other man I knew. Why, he happily changed diapers and gave you all baths. He was always holding you kids, singing songs. During your naps he would creep in on hands and knees, to peek into the crib and make sure you were breathing." I wanted to hear more about this wonderful daddy, about him and me in particular, but Mom always snapped out of these warm reveries abruptly.

With only four of us at home a pairing off of sorts became inevitable. My sister and father had their easy rapport so I gravitated toward my mother. I see now that was a bad thing. Dad simply wanted to get along with at least one of his children but Mom demanded an ally to whom she could pour out her grievances. Her constant chipping away at my dad made it all the harder for me to love him. Her wrath overwhelmed the warm side of her nature, erasing the infectious enthusiasm for life's million small pleasures that must have attracted my dad, fresh from his war, so many years ago. And she unwittingly drew a boundary that placed him and me on opposite sides.

There was no joy in being a daughter of this fractured union. But other than messing around with older men and drinking too much, I had no idea how to work an escape. It was always in the back of my mind that I would walk away someday. I had never taken any interest in decorating my bedroom, once I became the sole occupant, because I knew I was only passing through. I never brought friends to 101 PO because in my mind it was not a home but a battle zone, a place to flee from. Sometimes, asleep in my tiny bed, I dreamed I was a mist floating freely through the scenes of my life, remote and unstoppable, cool and serene.

Then it came time for college—my turn to bolt. My parents couldn't chip in for tuition and I couldn't yet cover my share so at the last minute I postponed for a year to save up. While my friends took off to become freshmen, I stayed in Branford and waitressed. That year my double life became more extreme. There was the diligent and responsible Julie, banking her paychecks, contributing financially at home, exercising diplomacy to help keep the bickering parents on an even keel. And there was the sneaky, elusive Julie, drinking more than ever and queuing up for birth control pills at Planned Parenthood.

Despite Dad's alert presence I continued my nocturnal carousing. Four or five nights a week I was a docile girl, reading or watching TV at home, going to bed at a respectable hour. But two or three nights I let loose. I would reel in after a dozen mixed drinks and go to bed in my clothes, having abandoned my nightgown ruse. At dawn I would awake perky and hangover free to rescue the car from some crazy perch—on the lawn, or nosing into Mom's garden—before my early-rising parents caught me in the act.

More than once I came home from New Haven bars after last call with a strange male at the wheel, with no memory in the morning of who he was or what had transpired once we got to 101 PO. After those nights I checked myself over nervously—Was my mouth swollen? My underwear in order? Another night I fell asleep at a boyfriend's apartment and woke to hear firemen breaking down the door. I raced outside, ignoring their shouts, to rescue my mother's car parked alongside the burning building. I drove around town for an hour with all the windows open but the next day the car still reeked of smoke. Mom didn't seem to notice, however, for which I thanked her Viceroy Longs.

One night she finally caught me stumbling in after four AM. As soon as I shut the door—softly, I thought—she came storming out of her bedroom. "Julia Mary!" she cried. "You're DRUNK!" Her outrage cut through my grogginess. Who was she to criticize? When she folded her arms and commanded me to walk a straight line I snapped back, "Oh, no. Nobody made YOU do that when I was little. All those times I found you lying on the floor, or in your room, passed out. So buzz off, Mom, please. I'm going to bed." My fury stunned her silent. In the morning I was clear eyed and alert, as usual. "I was hoping a good hangover would teach you a lesson," she muttered, banging dishes. She didn't dare go further. I caught my father appraising me but he said not a word.

When September finally arrived I was eager to leave for Dartmouth. As soon as I arrived, however, I realized how poorly I'd seen to my interests. I didn't warm to the sedately handsome buildings trimmed in "Dartmouth Green," the densely wooded terrain, the stifling valley. I was instantly homesick for the quick-changing light and imaginary infinity of the Sound. At night in my dorm I missed the familiar voice of my old friend the train passing through Branford. Dartmouth's hoary traditions and its privileged student body impressed on me just how poor my family really was. I had thought that once I left home my misfit days were over—but I was wrong.

During that first year, Mom sent me care packages—homemade cookies and more of those Connecticut Valley-style crocheted slippers—and frequent chatty letters. From my father I expected and heard nothing. I hoped he was okay. It had been a long time since I was privy to his secret thoughts. An important bond between us was fading, but part of me was glad. It was time for all Collinses to fend for themselves.

Slowly I collected a few good friends, fishes out of water like myself. The near two-to-one ratio of Dartmouth men to women spiked the social climate with tension but made it easy for me to pair up casually. I spent most weekends at parties—even the grotesque beer blitzes of Fraternity Row—dancing and drinking until morning, then reviving late the following afternoon. I realized I was flirting with a serious drinking problem but that didn't slow me. I wanted to drown my sense of inferiority and detachment, of being much too much like my dad. I started doing drugs too— acid, psychedelic mushrooms, pot, cocaine—something I'd always avoided. But booze was my preferred method of blanking out.

One Saturday I awoke to brisk knocking on my dorm room door. I lurched out of bed and tossed on my kimono. Fuzzy mouthed, half of my face imprinted from the pillow, my hair a rat's nest, I yanked open the door, mightily annoyed. A dark-haired stranger stood there, very clean-cut and L. L. Bean-looking. He appeared startled—dismayed actually —at the sight of me.

"Uh, am I too early? I thought I was supposed to pick you up at five."

"Yes, of course, come on in. Give me five minutes," I said, ushering him into my room as I broke into a nervous sweat. For I knew exactly what had happened. Clearly I'd met him at the party the night before and he asked me out before the alcohol short-circuited my brain. It didn't occur to me to confess: "Sorry, but I don't know who the hell you are so a date seems premature." Instead I hastily pulled myself together.

But after that night, I abruptly changed my ways. I had managed to alarm myself. I had also racked up too many other embarrassing incidents and felt my friends growing concerned over my behavior. From then on I invested more of myself in my classes and friendships and began to lighten inside, the long shadows of home finally pulling away. As if to reassure me the worst was over, that spring Dad's fortunes took an extraordinary turn. Armed with the world's worst resume he somehow wangled a new job with a small local insurance firm that offered a modest salary on top of commissions, plus exclusive use of a car, a pale-green late-model Ford. Dad was extremely proud of it. Cars had always been one of his few material interests. Now he had a good one, much fancier than Mom's tinny Toyota. He puffed up and acted a lot happier, the weekly checks utterly delighted my mother, and their relationship began to thaw.

The rest of my family was flourishing too. That summer my brother Peter married his girlfriend Laurel, the third resolute Collins son to brave the ritual at a young age. Jennifer and I sang at the wedding. Laurel had made her dress and Peter's wedding shirt, and she wore flowers in her hair.

Only a month later she was attacked and beaten unconscious at the U Conn running track, where she and Peter were grad students, and left in a bleeding heap. She had been out jogging on a sunny autumn morning. Her attacker was never caught. In a coma for weeks, when she awoke she had no idea who Peter was, nor anybody else she'd met since she'd been a teenager. I rushed home to her hospital bed and saw my sweet sister-in-law's misshapen face and Peter's anguish. My long run of willful self-destructiveness sickened me all the more, and I was disgusted by my parents' behavior. Mom made the attack into her own personal tragedy and Dad visited Laurel regularly but hid his feelings and offered no comfort to his son. He'd stayed on the sidelines too long now to take action as a parent.

My sister-in-law's condition improved at a rehab center but the long-term prognosis was dim. When the distant Time of Troubles had shattered our family I had thought that the worst had hit the Collinses. This new loss proved me wrong and our fumbling, incoherent support of Peter and Laurel made it plain we didn't know how to pull together. It seemed to me we were all infected with defeat and hopelessness, and I traced the contagion to my parents, especially Dad.

In January of my sophomore year I went to study in Toulouse, France. I felt guilty about my glorious opportunity. In my family only Dad had ever traveled so far. Mom still mourned her old dream of European travel, long ago put on ice by World War II. Dad hadn't left the States since the war took him across the equator, though he was apparently content to conduct his travels via the pages of *National Geographic*.

On the evening I was to fly to Paris, my first flight ever, my parents drove me to New Haven where a limo service would transport me to JFK Airport. I kept glancing at Mom to see if she was jealous beneath her show of gaiety, but couldn't tell. It wasn't till I climbed out of the car that I saw my dad's face. His eyes were bloodshot, his cheeks shiny from tears. I marveled at his emotion, amazed that I had caused it. "I wish you weren't going so far away, Chule," he whispered hoarsely as he hugged me goodbye. "It scares me. I have no idea what it's like over there. You take care, now. You keep safe." It struck me that he truly was afraid I might not make it back in one piece. What put that in his head? Wide awake for the entire transatlantic flight I kept finding his face in the inky window, overlaying my own reflection. For the first time since childhood he seemed to be watching over me. Certainly I knew it was all a fancy, that in reality he was probably lying in bed thinking of his war or his childhood, not of me. I was comforted anyway.

Every summer but one I returned to Branford to earn tuition money and police my parents, checking to see if their cease-fire was holding. The moment I walked in the door in early June my newly blossoming life instantly shrank to the dimensions of the low-ceilinged rooms in a dilapidated nineteenth-century farmhouse saturated with cigarette smoke and disappointment. The old betrayals and recriminations, the wounds from love and war, were always present and accounted for. Mom and Dad were aging into two old-timey characters like nobody else, their tense arrangement exacerbating their natural foibles till they resembled Thomas Wolfe's dysfunctional parents in *Look Homeward Angel*. After months away, I found I missed this dotty pair. But the long summer stretch of watchfulness put me in a state of constant irritation. When I observed my sister, the last college-bound Collins, anticipating her imminent release, I wondered why I still felt shackled.

During these bumpy months the Fourth of July was the day I dreaded most, the predictable low point of summer when Dad's anguish over the war inevitably resurfaced. The patriotic hoopla stirred up his most cynical associations, his caustic responses to the pro-America stories in the *New Haven Register* and on TV reflecting his great divide between pride and bitterness over his Marine service.

When I was tiny, barely at the stage of forming lasting memories, Dad used to take our family to Branford Point to watch the annual fireworks display. But once my parents' marriage hit the skids, we stopped going for good and I could tell he was relieved. I also didn't mind giving up the outing because the fireworks upset me. Dad taught me early to associate them with the murderous explosions of war. So many times he had obsessively described the varieties of artillery and mortars he'd met as a Marine, how they'd wailed and keened and howled and shrieked, gouging and scalping the earth, shearing human heads and limbs. He recalled with rapt horror the mass raids by kamikaze, their exploding bombs and gas tanks combining with the American fleet's ferocious defense into spectacular kabooms. At the Branford fireworks he tensed up when a barrage of nasty little "screamer" rockets writhed and screeched their way into the Sound. He was even wary around sparklers, our tame substitute—how it would agitate him when Jennifer and I made the sizzling, spitting wands dance in the backyard darkness, squealing at the raining sparks! "Careful, careful, JESUS! DON'T DROP IT JULIE, be careful girls," he pleaded. One year, when a neighbor set off a particularly loud explosive, Dad threw himself to the ground screaming, "Hit the deck!"

Then we outgrew sparklers. Dad stopped taking Miff and me to the parade. Friends and relatives no longer came over. A trip to the beach was out of the question—in the post-Mrs. Ketchum period we never set foot on Branford Point again. After the Time of Troubles, all that remained of our former July Fourth pomp was the suppertime menu: barbecued chicken, corn on the cob, and blueberry pie. Each year Dad quietly manned the grill, charring the meat as the flames lapped up the "secret" barbecue sauce recipe he'd learned from Pop. We ate quickly and quietly, indoors, listening to kids playing Marco Polo in a swimming pool across the way, music blaring from a radio, the uproar of family get-togethers in neighboring backyards. Our own festivities were over before dusk.

On the last Fourth of July before I graduated from Dartmouth I knew something was seriously wrong at home. When I arrived at the start of the summer, the changes in my parents alarmed me. Both were aging dramatically, the evidence of their fractious lives catching up with them all at once, spoiling the remains of what had been, in each, abundant good looks. At fifty-nine Mom looked exhausted and her skin and eyes were dull. It didn't help that she'd settled on the worst hairdresser at the cheap-cuts parlor, who colored her pixielike style a brassy shade that did battle with her slightly sallow complexion. Dad fared better overall but his teeth were rotting and he refused to see a dentist, so he chewed carefully and rarely smiled. He had also acquired a troubling cough.

Even more disturbing, Mom was turning on Dad again, despite his slim but steady earnings, whipping him with unwarranted complaints and criticisms. He warded her off with a smart-ass remark or two and then fled to his room, upset and depressed. Sometimes I intervened and she baffled me by immediately backing off. "Let's just drop it, shall we?" she said with fake gaiety. "Jerry, Julie's on your side so I'll shut up now."

I already knew what Dad thought was the matter; he'd broached his fear in the car, when I came home for a weekend during the spring. I had brushed him off at the time, too petrified to let in the truth. No, it can't be, I insisted vehemently. A few trivial lapses, that was all. "I'm telling you, she's out of control," he pressed, close to tears. "And I can't go through this all over again, Julie." He banged his palm on the steering wheel, his bony back rigid with misery. "It's all right, Dad," I said coldly. "I really think you're making too much of it." After that I shut him down if he even hinted at what was going on.

On that particular Fourth, we dined earlier than usual. It was an overcast day with a white-hot sky and no breeze. Nothing moved unless it had to. The birds twittered weakly. The leaves on the trees looked burnt. Dad manned the grill, leaving the meat on too long. Mom had husked the corn, making quite a racket at it, but the cooked ears were still lined with silk that took a while to pick off. She had undercooked the potatoes and her blueberry pie was a sorry mess, runny inside with a cracked and blackened crust. My sister was gone for the day, sensibly choosing to beat it and avoid our tightly wound affair. As we three doggedly masticated that unhappy meal I felt a familiar warning buzz begin to spread throughout my body. I looked at Mom, who barely said a word. She was scowling at her plate. I met my father's eyes across the table and he nodded slightly, his mouth a flat unhappy line.

That night I hunkered down in the doorway of my childhood bedroom, listening with all my might, exactly as I had a dozen years before. Everyone had gone to bed except my sister, who was still out with friends. Dad was awake; I knew he was worrying. Mom was awake, too; I could sense her longing. She occupied Angy's old room on the first floor, and a few feet away from me there was an ancient heat register in the hallway that carried any sounds from her bedroom below. If my mother had been thinking clearly she would have shut it, because it could not be opened without a loud warning rasp.

Suddenly I heard that icy clink. For a moment I wanted to bawl, a panicky seven year old all over again. Then the rage took over—I had never felt anything like it. In one ferocious leap I was on my feet and flying down the stairs, hurling around the corner into my mother's room with weightless ease, the vengeful ghost of a broken-hearted child. Mom was sitting up in her bed, a glass in one hand, jumbo vodka bottle in the other. "Ohhhhhh," she breathed, a Marilyn Monroe-like cooing. In the dimness her face was oddly youthful, smooth and lovely again, her strange-colored hair returned to its original dark shade. I found her eyes, two steady beams of unbearable deception. "Julie. Darling." She was already working up her excuses, in which Dad would figure prominently. "Oh, Julie," she sighed deeply, still holding her glass and her bottle tightly.

"How dare you," I began but the rest of my tirade doesn't matter. In the morning Mom was fresh as the early sunlight, ready with her heartfelt apology and eloquent explanation. "I promise, Julie," she said over and over with wide-eyed sincerity. "I swear it. Never again." That morning I scrutinized Dad more closely than I had in a long time. I saw the weary combat veteran girding up for another day in hell. His war was never over.

CHAPTER TWELVE NIGHT WATCH

Young Blanche Gutfinski shortly before her marriage to Jerry Collins

When the lights go on again
All over the world
And the boys are home again
All over the world
And rain or snow is all that may fall from the skies above
A kiss won't mean "goodbye" but "hello to love"...

("When the Lights Go on Again")

When he first joined the Marines Jerry Collins hit the sack as often and for as long as possible. Sleep was one of the few luxuries left to a working Leatherneck. But on Okinawa, the booming guns, wailing shells, the shouts and screams of men on both sides went on and on. Nobody slept on Okinawa.

Fighting in the open, exposed to sniper fire and artillery, the Marines abruptly learned that survival was a moment-by-moment proposition. By day, however, the imperative to keep moving and support one's comrades distracted them from notions of imminent death. Nighttime was a different story. "Slow torture," Dad called it. It was unsafe to move about. Fear came hunting for the Marines holed up in their foxholes and makeshift shelters.

At night the invisible enemy soldiers shouted taunts across the line: "Sleep well, Yankee dogs. Tomorrow you all die." Dad was haunted most by the jeers he couldn't make out, in Japanese. I know a couple of these mysterious threats by heart because he often repeated them, reliving his cold unease at the sound of hostile voices hissing in the dark.

When the worst of Okinawa was over, Dad reverted to the hearty sleeper he'd been, making up for months of exhaustion. Later, however, when he returned to the states, he suddenly stopped sleeping through the night. Sometimes he snapped alert with a jolt, imagining himself back in the middle of conflict. He bolted out of bed, frantic to abandon his foxhole, to get out of the area. Other times he lay trapped in his dream, imagining an enemy soldier creeping nearer while he was pinned in place. On the worst nights he woke while scrambling for his weapon as the enemy leaped into his hole.

Dad's troubled nights continued after his marriage and the births of his sons. By the time I arrived a pattern was set that lasted till the end of his life. As a child I was often awakened by familiar sounds coming from my parents' bedroom: Dad coughing and clearing his throat, the bedsprings complaining when he got up to go downstairs, the weary floorboards reporting his every move. Occasionally I tiptoed after him, to hide by the open doorway and watch him standing at the kitchen counter, his back toward me, motionless except for the tiny comet of his cigarette tip traveling up to his mouth and down to his side, over and over, his self-soothing ritual.

Even then I knew better than to disturb him. It reassured me to observe my daddy for a minute or two while he inhaled and sighed and cleared his throat, unaware of my presence, before I crept back upstairs and finally went to sleep.

As I grew older his night prowling saddened me, because I knew the kinds of thoughts that crowded around him in the dark. Sometimes I joined him downstairs, unable to bear the idea of him lurking alone. Our nocturnal meetings were invariably awkward; I never knew whether he welcomed my company.

"How's the night watch?" I would ask.

"Two AM and all is well. Can't sleep, Chule?"

"No. Too restless."

"Me too. I had a bad dream."

"About what?"

"Ooo-hoo-hoo-hoo," he gave an exaggerated shudder, trying to be playful. "I'd rather not get into it. It's fading anyway."

I never told him about my own nightmares—exploding pineapples, a muddy hill covered with body parts, dead people with their eyes wide open staring at the sky. He was the one who needed protecting. I poured myself a glass of milk or made some hot cocoa, sipping while he smoked until I grew bored and sleepy and left him to finish his Kools.

Both of my parents had started smoking during the war years. Mom was a ladylike smoker who concealed all traces with fastidious hygiene, Listerine, and perfume, while Dad was cured and reeking like an honest slab of bacon, his skin and hair and clothing saturated with tobacco. I didn't mind. The aroma of old butts was a comforting eau de Dad. And I knew his "cigs" were his lifeline during those vulnerable, solitary hours when his war memories slaughtered his sleep.

✻ ✻ ✻

Dear Julie,

I'm sorry you had to see what's going on with your mother. I'm sure it has made you very unhappy. But now you know I'm not making it up. In fact, she is getting worse. I am keeping an eagle eye on her, to determine when and how much she is drinking but now that she knows we're both on to her she is doing her best to hide all the traces. I wouldn't drag any of you kids into this except your mother is sick and not herself anymore. I don't think she has started drinking on the job yet but it is only a matter of time. I may need your help, Julie. I don't think I can go it alone. Nothing I say makes a difference to her. In fact, sometimes it makes things worse and gives her an excuse to drink more. I think she would listen to you kids. However I don't think I can ask your brothers to jump in at this time and Jennifer is too young....

That's the gist of a letter I got from Dad in September of my senior year in college, after that Fourth of July when I caught Mom with her bottle and begrudgingly accepted what my scout-observer Dad had deduced after her first sip. I was amazed when I pulled an envelope from my mailbox and saw his careful schoolboy script. It was the first letter I'd gotten from him since he'd sent those coded dispatches from a New Haven flophouse.

I sped through the pages, the bad news striking out at me. Mom was out of control, and Dad was calling desperately for reinforcements. I started to tear up his letter, enraged. How could she do this again? How dare he look to me to bail him out? My parents had made their choices, so let them deal with the consequences.

In the end, however, pity and duty won out. I put down the letter and called home. Mom answered and launched into frenetic, disarming chitchat before I finally interrupted: "I need to speak to Dad."

"Oh! Okay. He's right here, darling."

"Hello, Chule?" He sounded nervous.

"Hi, Dad. I got your letter. I understand the situation. I can't come home this month but I promise I will in a few weeks. Keep me posted, okay?"

"You betcha! Let us know when you're coming!" His bright tone meant Mom was hovering. "Jerry, let me talk to her again," she said in the background, cutting him short. As she came back on the line my heart sank. I could tell she was suspicious. Her guard was up. We were in for it, all right.

During my final semester I treated my course work like so many monotonous rows to hoe, and managed to finish college magna cum laude, Phi Beta Kappa, and utterly purposeless. While classmates made plans for grad school, internships, management training programs, the Peace Corps, a year of travel, I felt frozen, unable to envision any desirable course of action and distracted by my fears about what was going on at home.

At night my dreams began replaying lurid old scenes from our Time of Troubles. Even by day I felt weighted down with dread. Dad's letters grew shorter, more urgent. The old OCS flunkout was looking to me to come up with the plan. In four years away from home I'd slowly developed a good life on my own. But as graduation approached I avoided friends, skipped the special dinner for honors thesis writers and the Phi Beta Kappa ceremony, stopped attending all social events, and started shedding my belongings. I was lightening my load, preparing to isolate myself.

Graduation day was appropriately grim. A steady rainfall made Dartmouth's natural splendors look like hell. When my parents and sister finally drove up I saw right away that Mom had broken all of her effusive promises to me. She was tense and twitchy and looked under the weather, all obvious signs, as was her messy makeup. After the ceremony my tiny entourage went out for lunch and she promptly ordered wine.

"Mom, what are you doing," I yelped, appalled. My sister and father exchanged glances. Mom's decision that she could handle a little "social drinking" wasn't news to them.

"I'm entitled," she snapped. "Don't you say another word about it, Julie. I'm an adult. There's no problem here." She changed the subject immediately, expressing heated annoyance that I had not graduated wearing a Phi Beta Kappa ribbon on my robe because I'd played hooky when they gave them out. But the cowardly look was back in her eyes. That told me the bottle was in command and could make her do anything—lie, deceive, connive, even piss all over her daughter's big day. And still she would arise forgetful and serene the following morn, to dash off a note to the *Branford Review* trumpeting my academic achievements.

Over the next few years I moved to New York City where I did a short stint as a paralegal, to Boston where I worked at a publishing house, then back to New York where I attended journalism school. My sister was in college now, which meant my parents were alone together at last. Days I attended class and crisscrossed the city on assignments, and nights I temped to pay my tuition. One weekend each month I forced myself to train home to Connecticut where I found Mom lurching toward the brink and Dad growing haggard from constant vigilance.

He sent me regular correspondence from the front line. I also gauged the state of things from the handwriting in my mother's letters, which slowly disintegrated into a frail, tremulous scrawl, the words stumbling off the page or vanishing midsentence. Then she stopped writing or calling altogether and I knew the free fall had begun.

For a while Mom had tried to stave off binging: she kept on working, saving her drinking till she was alone in her bedroom at night, then freshening up like mad in the morning. Soon she began spiriting a little something in her purse to the office, to mix with orange juice on coffee breaks. Once active in the Yale union movement, she took to griping about its demands on her time. Always popular with grad students and professors, she stopped taking an interest in them or her colleagues. Before long she was dissuading friends from visiting the house. The cutely panhandling neighborhood children were no longer welcome, either, as Mom metamorphosed in their eyes from that nice lady who gives treats to the scary wild-eyed witch. After that she began staying in her room for longer periods, spending most of Saturday and Sunday lying in bed, her glass never empty. Soon she was skipping Mondays too, then calling in sick for days at a time. When Dad tried to intervene, she flung things at him, raising lumps and bruises.

The five Collins children were scattered around the country, but we all felt the same foreboding. I was the closest to home, working as a freelancer in Boston after grad school, so I continued my trips to Branford, trying to keep Mom in check and Dad from despair. Each visit left me reeling and sometimes I resisted making them, postponing until Dad couldn't take it. "Will you really come this time?" he begged. "Please, Julie."

The situation worsened when his steady employment ended with a bang. His company car was taken away and the IRS renewed its zealous hounding. Perhaps he was fired for the usual reasons: missing a quota, spending too many hours daydreaming over his files. However he was also no longer an attractive emissary for any company: he was still tall and slim but his teeth were falling out and he had coughing jags at inconvenient moments. Even when I cajoled him—Dad, I'm worried, maybe this is emphysema—he adamantly refused to get medical care.

Dad's firing made him financially dependent again on his ex-wife. She promptly lost her own job, having drained the near bottomless patience of her kind boss. Terrified by the specter of poverty, Mom briefly went into detox and cleaned her act up enough to reclaim her job, deploying her disarming charm. Then the package store started delivering again. She had a couple fender benders. One night she drank herself unconscious, still clutching a lit cigarette. My insomniac father rushed in to pull away the burning bedding. The next time it was a charred chair. Her housekeeping efforts left a trail of broken glass and pottery. She began cooking with wine and sherry, till everything tasted soused. She reverted to her old habits: hiding a bottle in the clothes dryer, behind the sofa, up in the attic, stowing sticky glasses in the garden, behind cereal boxes, in the cellar, stuck in the bookcases.

Dad gradually took over the errands and cooking, to keep Mom off the road and away from the stove. When she stopped getting out of bed altogether he became her nurse, washing the sheets and blankets she soiled, trying to coax her to eat something, to drink a little water instead of her favorite fluids.

His eyes were perpetually bloodshot. Many nights he gave up sleeping altogether, fearing she would start another fire and kill them both. He spent hours sitting at the top of the stairs, listening to Blanche bartending in her bedroom, muttering and singing nonsense till at last she fell silent, stupefied, until the middle of the next day.

One afternoon he telephoned me. His voice was curt and businesslike: "Julie, you had better come home. As fast as you can." It sounded like an order.

When I walked into 101 PO, Mom immediately rushed at me waving a fry pan. I recoiled, shocked by her swollen and discolored face, the stink of her flapping bathrobe.

"Get out of my house!" she shrieked. "Who invited you? Leave me alone!"

My head snapped to one side, a starburst of pain blinding me. I dropped to my knees on the linoleum, flabbergasted. My own mother had hit me!

I passed out as Dad came tearing into the room. No more than a minute or two went by, however, because when I came to he was still shouting. "Jesus Christ, Blanche! Look what you've done!" He'd wrested the pan away from her and forced her into a chair. She sat there glowering. Then she burst into yawping sobs.

I got on my feet, my skull still clanging. "Stay still, Mom. I'm going to get you some coffee and a snack. You'll feel better, I promise."

Dad handed me a hand towel wrapped around some ice. "I'll make it for her. You put this on your head. We'd better get you to a doctor."

"No, I'm fine." And I decided I was. I studied myself in the mirror, gingerly patting my cranium.

All at once she was up again, barreling past me to the telephone. "Enough already! I'm calling the Cork Shop," she shouted, defiantly. "And nobody has the right to stop me."

Dad lunged and grabbed her hand on the receiver. "Please, Blanche. Give the drinking a rest, for God's sake. You just clobbered your own daughter."

She began flailing at him. Together he and I pushed her backward into her room and shut the door. I told him to make sure she stayed put while I called for an ambulance.

"I will never, never, never forgive you," Mom hissed as the EMTs strapped her onto the gurney and wheeled her outside. Once inside the ambulance my mother craned her neck to find me and aim a lethal glare. "Do you hear me, Julia Mary Collins? Do you hear me, Jerry, you bastard? I will NEVER forgive you."

Dad and I followed the ambulance to the emergency room, where we begged the staff to keep her for a few days, till she sobered enough so I could persuade her to enter a program voluntarily. At last one of the doctors agreed.

We couldn't face home right away, so I treated Dad to dinner out. I couldn't recall the last time we'd been alone together away from 101 PO. Fathers and daughters often enjoy each other's company, I thought. One-on-one, having a nice, easygoing time, no big deal. Why hadn't we ever? Why was our connection based on painful things? Yet our dinner conversation was mostly cheerful that evening, light-headed with the relief of knowing Mom was in good hands and—I'll admit it—out of the way for a while.

Back at the house we sat at the kitchen table for a long spell, savoring the peace. We talked about Mom, what might lie ahead, and how the rest of the family was doing before moving on to a safe, easy topic: the state of the town we both loved. Branford was drifting Republican after many decades as a Democratic stronghold, and we launched into a satisfying tear on that, with Dad filling me in on the current ne'er-do-wells responsible for the condo boom and development projects that threatened to destroy what remained of the town's rural character. "You should be first selectman, Dad," I said, remembering how he nearly ran for the office years before. He looked pleased. For that moment both of us believed it could have happened, and I remembered how proud I once was of my dad. He had stood out in the crowd, his head held high, his expression knowing and bemused—a noteworthy man.

He went to get more Kools and I unsettled him by asking for one. "Gee, I didn't know you smoked, Julie. That doesn't seem like a good idea," he frowned. "My lungs have had it but yours are still young."

I laughed at him. "I'm not starting a habit, Dad. I only want one." I burned my way through one harsh Kool, imitating his languid smoking style.

It got so late he urged me to go to bed. "I'll turn in soon, too."

Half an hour or later I was back downstairs, however, too jittery to conk out. I found him smoking in the kitchen, at his customary post, with all the lights turned off.

"Jesus, Dad. Don't you EVER sleep?" It distressed me that he wasn't taking advantage of Mom's absence to get some rest. Even after a decent meal I'd noticed how wasted he appeared. Not much was left of my once-dashing dad.

"I don't need much sleep," he said edgily. "It's been that way since the war. I've told you that before, Julie. And lately, with your mother— "

"Dad, if she doesn't get better come stay with me a while," I blurted impetuously, even as I cringed inside at the prospect. He seemed so desolate, worn out from years of skirmishing with an impossible woman he couldn't or wouldn't leave.

"Thanks, Chule. We'll see." He would never take me up on the offer, however, not unless Mom burned the house to the ground. She had always been too much for him—full of impossible expectations and unmerciful rage, blind to the effects of her addiction and his lingering war. Nonetheless, this oddest of couples had stuck together, one way or another, for more than three decades.

He took a last long drag and ground out his cigarette. "Beddy-bye time. It's nearly four o'clock already."

We kissed goodnight. I climbed into bed and stared at the ceiling, knowing he was awake too. I stretched and sighed, knowing that in the morning he would begin to irritate me all over again with his passivity, his failing health, his reliance on me to figure out how to handle Mom. I would wish myself beyond the reach of his pleading letters and calls.

A car came rushing along Pine Orchard Road, slowing as it approached our house. I sat up in bed, my heart accelerating. Gravel scattered as the car ran up to our side door and stopped, the engine still chugging with the raggedy rhythm of poor maintenance. There was a long pause and then a door slammed, much too loud for the hour.

"Oh, no," I heard my father moan, as the car sped backward on the driveway and took off the way it had come.

The kitchen door was unlocked, as always, but our visitor struggled to open it, making an unholy racket. I heard slow footsteps in the kitchen, the sound of something heavy dragging over the linoleum. I thought of Marley's Ghost from *A Christmas Carol*, hauling his self-made chains. Thump-thump-thump—it was that heavy leather handbag—accompanied by a low-pitched monotonous ranting in an ugly voice I'd never heard before. It gave me gooseflesh.

"And they started screaming," it droned, "and I was trapped, strapped down, listening to them scream, the screaming-meemie heebie-jeebies. Bodies everywhere, making noises. And the smell—like nothing else on earth. Help, come get me, I begged. Get me out of here. I begged and I pleaded and nobody came. Well, if nobody will save me then I guess I'm on my own." The voice turned triumphant. "They couldn't keep me, no sir! I sashayed right on out of there!"

I got out of bed and glided to the top of the stairs. My father was already there, in a furtive listening pose, one hand on the wall to steady himself as he leaned over the top steps to hear better. "It's your mother," he whispered. Then, with compressed fury, "Listen to her! Drunk as ever! She must have had some in her purse—she fills cough syrup bottles. How could those idiot doctors let her leave? What on god's earth do we do now?"

"JERRY!" The jump in volume made us both start. I grabbed my father's shoulder to steady him. "JERRY! I KNOW YOU'RE UP THERE!" Then low again, mumbling, "So you thought you'd get rid of me, you thought I was gone for good, why you bastard. Well, ha, ha, ha, nothing doing, you— " she spat out a string of curses I never could have imagined issuing from my eloquent, ex-English-teacher mom. Her voice faded, then grew loud again. "YOU HAVE SOME NERVE JERRY COLLINS!" Another pause. "YOU OWE ME FOR THAT DAMN TAXI! AND I GAVE THE NICE DRIVER A WHOPPING TIP!"

Dad was shivering uncontrollably. "Oh god, oh god, oh god. Christ almighty. Jesus, Mary, and Joseph." For a man with no religion left he dropped a lot of names. I found his right hand and squeezed it. My initial horror was subsiding as something else took over—an aloof resignation. Through the nearest bedroom window I could see the sky turning pale. I wished myself on the beach, watching sky and water separate as the horizon brightened while the salt air patted my cheek the way Mom used to do.

Thump-thump-thump—silence. She'd finally let go of her handbag. Her vocal chords worn out, she shut up at last. We listened to her shamble from the kitchen to the dining room, pausing to rummage noisily, knocking things over. She was looking for a bottle but had forgotten where she'd stashed any. She bumped an antique cast-iron toy, a circus wagon with a tiger inside, and it rolled off an end table, landing with a terrible bang. "Oh, dear," she sighed, sounding for a moment like her real self.

Now I could almost make out my father's profile, that obstinate nose. He took a deep breath, adopting a casual tone. Like me, he'd observed it would be morning soon. The night watch was over. "Well, here we go again, Chule. I'm going to get dressed and head downstairs. I'll look after her. You'd better get some sleep before it's broad daylight."

"Forget that, Dad. We're in this together." Saving Mom was a hopeless mission, and we both knew it, but I would share it with him.

CHAPTER THIRTEEN HOMECOMING

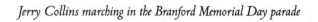

Jerry Collins marching in the Branford Memorial Day parade

Blackbird, blackbird, singing the blues all day.
Right outside of my door.
Blackbird blackbird why do you sit and say
There's no sunshine in store
All through the winter you hung around
Now I begin to feel homeward bound
Blackbird blackbird gotta be on my way where there's sunshine galore.

("Bye Bye Blackbird")

While Cpl. Jerry Collins twiddled his thumbs in China the victory celebrations wound down in the states and the country turned its attention away from war. Throughout the frigid winter of '46 he waited for replacements to arrive in Tsingtao so he could be cleared for departure. His letters grew shorter, afire with impatience. "I'm so anxious to see you that I almost burst," he wrote his parents.

Then all at once Jerry's number was up. He mailed his last letter from China on March 16, rejoicing that he would soon board a ship for California. The cheerful boy of boot camp made a brief, ecstatic comeback: "I've millions of things to tell you and to ask and gillions to do. It will certainly be swell to be home where I have a room of my own and my mother and father again."

The April 15th edition of the *New Haven Evening Register*, the Collins family's big-city paper, reported that "Mr. and Mrs. J. J. Collins of Pine Orchard Road have received word of the arrival of their son, Jerry, at San Diego, Calif., returning from Tangtao [sic], China. Corporal Collins has completed more than three years service with the Marines and has been in the Pacific area more than two years with the Sixth Marine Division, which was in combat on Okinawa."

Waiting at the San Diego dock to greet Jerry's troopship *Lubbock* were neither Lana Turner nor Rita Hayworth nor Betty Grable, but the dashingly macabre Bela Lugosi who played Dracula in the movies. Lugosi welcomed the Marines in his best batlike style, striking debonair poses, swooping and flapping his famous cape. Later Dad told me he and his shipmates picked Dracula to meet them instead of the usual Hollywood starlet, because they wanted to broadcast loud and clear: Who cares about cheesecake? Enough is enough already! We've done our time! Let us go home!

During processing in San Diego, Cpl. Collins learned that his regiment, the Twenty-ninth, had been awarded the Presidential Unit citation and Navy Unit citation. He also got a good conduct medal. No Purple Heart, however. He'd come through unscathed except for typical souvenirs of Okinawa and the tropics: shrapnel and jungle-rot scarring, respiratory ailments, dental problems, and a skulking malaria that would flare up over the years, the latter leaving me with memories of a yellow-skinned daddy with the shakes. He received no medals for individual heroism—he quietly exited the war as an unsung working Leatherneck who'd risked himself alongside countless others.

He'd also missed out on that sergeant stripe he'd worked toward for so long, which he'd been told was coming shortly before he shipped out. No matter: "My blouse sports two rows of ribbons and stars, which don't mean a thing compared to the pleasure of changing into civilian clothes," he told his "folksies." Next he was shuttled on to Bainbridge, Maryland, where Serial Number 509069 received his honorable discharge on April 18 and enough money for a one-way ticket home. Keep your fingers crossed, he wrote, and I just might show up in time for Easter dinner.

With that the diligent military correspondent retired his pen at last. Jerry was done with his war. Or so it seemed.

Since it made Dad melancholy to relive it, I have to conjure that triumphant day he finally rolled into Branford—his anticipation as the taxi crested the shady hill on Pine Orchard Road signaling the home stretch, the clutch at his throat when he saw the pleasant farmhouse in its peaceful garden setting, his ecstatic parents hurrying out to the driveway to embrace him. Angy and Pop surely cooked up one of the sumptuous feasts Jerry had day-dreamed of while dining from his mess kit on "shit on a shingle" and other canine-style delights. With a cigar stuck in his mouth, Pop fired up the grill for those famous "charcoal specials" his son had craved on Guadalcanal, or maybe Angy served up one of her juicy roasts with potatoes and the winter root vegetables her boy liked so much. She would have baked her fancy dinner rolls and a devil's food cake for dessert. The homemade brew, or harder stuff, must have flowed. "Schwester" bustled over from her own little apartment and Jerry finally met Bill Sadowski, whom his sister had married soon after he arrived in Tsingtao. Jerry's "brother" Brownie the cocker spaniel was also on hand. So were Uncle Den and Aunt Nellie, and perhaps Aunt Dollie and Uncle Nicholas, Aunt Mildred and Uncle Freddy, and assorted cousins.

Aside from Chinese silk and figurines, and some nifty Marine gear he planned to share around, Jerry hadn't bothered with much in the way of souvenirs—no enemy helmet or pistol or sword or flag and none of the ghoulish artifacts some combat vets took home. He had his medals, his knife, and his precious photos including candids of his buddies, many now dead or recovering from serious wounds, plus a high-gloss portrait of FDR and a pensive mug shot of himself taken in China. Most important of all he had about a thousand dollars saved up in war bonds and military pay; that money and the GI Bill were to set him on the road to his Ph.D. and a career as a research scientist pursuing humanitarian goals at the lofty Rockefeller Foundation.

After gorging on home cooking and unpacking his duffels, Jerry reclaimed his former room: a snug cubby plainly furnished with a leather chair, a bookcase full of his old schoolbooks, and a twin-sized bed too short for a full-grown vet. As he lay awake his brain must have spun with all that had happened since he last slept at home. I wonder if, despite the reassuring sameness of 101 PO, he already had any inkling, any trepidation about how radically the ground had shifted under his feet since the telegram summoned him to Parris Island in 1943. Did he guess that his experiences might not let him comfortably slip back into his prewar self, because nothing could possibly fit the same anymore? Did he notice that the comforts he had missed so acutely, the goals he had cherished, the sense of purpose he thought defined him were all strangely less compelling than he'd expected? Was he aware yet that even his love for his family was under a shadow because they had become "them," naive and oblivious beneficiaries of the war, while he was part of "us," the fighting forces who had endured its torments? Exactly when did my father begin to feel the big letdown familiar to countless vets?

As Jerry settled in he would have called on his faithful former pen pals, including little John Shirk who had prayed for him, a rather grand "old Virginny" lady named Mrs. Proffitt who drove him nuts with her doting, and "Mac" MacCarthy and other boyhood friends who'd survived the war. He speedily renewed his precious driver's license, commandeering one of the two Collins cars to go joyriding about the local roads that had been quiet lanes free of stop signs or traffic lights when he left for boot camp, and now buzzed with new cars and people on the go. Master of his own destiny once more, Dad must have loved the feel of the wheel under his hands. Hitting the road began to tempt him far more than hitting his chemistry texts.

Soon after his return he briefly commanded the spotlight when he put on his dress greens and led a parade down Branford's Main Street. My sister now keeps the blurry antique snapshot of Cpl. Collins smartly striding past the Horowitz Brothers department store. Dad's posture and grooming are impeccable, a credit to the

Marines. But his head is turned to eye the photographer, who must have yelled to grab his attention. The Marine's wry smirk seems to say, "This is pretty silly but all the same I'm standing here and you're on the sidewalk. You soft civilians don't know what I know."

After that day he shucked his military duds to don a sports jacket, ready to step into the future he'd obsessively planned for three years. But he never got there. After an aborted return to grad school and a fast-moving love affair with Blanche Gutfinski, Jerry took that cruddy industrial-chemist job in New Jersey. He barely lasted a year before he quit and convinced his pregnant wife to return to Branford, where he promptly embarked on a course of slow and steady defeat.

* * *

Pack up all my care and woe
Here I go singing low
Bye, bye blackbird.
Where somebody waits for me
Sugar's sweet so is she
Bye, bye blackbird.
Ain't nobody else can understand me
O what hard luck stories they all hand me.
Make my bed and light the light
I'll arrive late tonight
Blackbird bye bye.

Near the end of his life Dad got one last chance to shake off his World War II demons and finally live in peace. But not before Mom nearly did them both in.

In the winter of 1989, when it seemed she and her bottle were one at last, the blood in her veins replaced by vodka, my mother became shockingly ill. She was rushed to the hospital near death. By then Dad was tottering from fatigue, his diet reduced to cigarettes, canned food, and coffee. Weeks of round-the-clock vigilance had left him on the edge of collapse.

A top surgeon saved Mom but this last binge had taken a serious toll. It wasn't certain if she would recover. She couldn't eat or drink for months. The hospital johnny exposed stringy discolored arms and withered thighs. Yet even in her wrecked state, the star of grand rounds managed to woo the medical students with her outsized personality and charm, grown bold and a touch bawdy with age. Whenever Dad and I visited, Mom trundled about the ward with her IV cart and her cup of ice chips, forcing us to trot along as she chatted up the other patients.

Dad and I took advantage of our phoenix's enforced sobriety to brave the *A* word again, risking a feeble echo of her violent wrath. "You're an alcoholic, Blanche. You've got to know now you can never take another drink," he told her with uncharacteristic sternness while I stood there nodding, before wielding my own hammer: "Mom, this was as close a call as it gets. You nearly died. I counted the vodka bottles in your room, you know, so please don't give me any bullshit about how you wound up here." She stared back at us, wide eyed and accepting. During her long hospitalization, once and only once did Mom refer to herself as an alcoholic but that was all it took to send my hopes rocketing. She admitted it! She said *the word*.

After her discharge from the hospital, an extraordinary change came over my parents. They immediately gave up fighting and formed a new partnership, one I would never fully understand. It was Mom who reported these astonishing developments to me. She was weak as a chick so Dad did most of the cooking and shopping and chauffeured her around town. It turned out he liked to cook, Mom wrote, praising his beef stew. "Delicious! I'll get him to make it for you when you come next time." Slowly she either forgave or shelved the old betrayals. They began joking and gossiping together, rediscovering how much they had in common. I saw glimmers of what had brought them together in the first place.

Somehow my parents had survived their slugfest. They'd stuck together into their midsixties, long enough to celebrate a fantastic milestone: Dad was now a respectable retirement age. Mom encouraged him to give up his feeble efforts to rekindle his sales career and start collecting Social Security—more money per month than he had ever known. That first government check was the key to his prison cell, freeing him from decades of shame as a Marine who for all his brains and schemes never made the grade in the postwar world. And as soon as Mom gathered enough strength and chutzpah to ask for her own job back, between them, by Collins standards, they were rolling in dough. Mom bought herself the genuine Coach handbag she'd always coveted, and Dad got his first new suit in years. She had the living room and dining room carpeted and repapered and he finally went in for a new pair of eyeglasses. As long as he didn't smile and expose his bad teeth he looked pretty damn good for a man of his age.

For as long as I could remember my father had no friends. I'd always thought he was the loneliest man in the world. But with Mom back at Yale and needing him less at home, and freed from the pretense of chasing success, he suddenly burst out of his isolation to socialize with a small group of Branford men, some of them fellow vets. They met for coffee every day at Friendly's, "to solve the world's problems," Dad said. Occasionally when I was in town I spotted Mom's car in the parking lot and knew he was inside, shooting the breeze with his buddies. They nicknamed him "the General." We called his grey-haired posse "the A-Bay Gang" because they stationed themselves in the section at the front of the store, to monitor all comings and goings. One of the guys, Dino, was a particular favorite of Dad's. An amateur painter, he gave my father a watercolor of a Branford seagull coming in for a landing over the salt marsh among some towering cattails. Dad treasured it.

My visits home became less frequent and a lot happier. During one, my mother said she wanted me to see something. "Look at this," she said, unfolding a small piece of paper. "It's a love letter from your father."

When I was a child she had showed me the *billet-doux* Dad wrote to her before their marriage, bound with a sentimental pink ribbon, and pulled one out to read aloud. It was a touching letter, old-fashioned in its simple, straightforward pledges of devotion. Plainly Jerry Collins loved Blanche Gutfinski very much. Later on, when I was a teenager, Mom informed me angrily that she had thrown all of the letters away: "I couldn't stand to have them around any more. They turned out to be a pack of lies."

Now I read the note she held up in her callused, elderly farm-girl fingers. "Dear Blanche," it said. "You're a royal pain in the ass but I love you. I'm grateful that you're well and we are getting along again. I will do anything to keep it that way. All my love, Jerry." While I compared this succinct snippet to Dad's more effusive ardor of the late forties, my mother waited for my reaction. I think I said "Wow." I felt awkward glimpsing private warmth between my parents, spying on my dad's feelings. "A royal pain in the ass but I love you"—under the circumstances, after all the hate-filled years, John Donne couldn't have put it better. Mom tossed me a bright smile and went to put the note away in her desk. The astonishing possibility that my parents might remarry crossed my mind. I dismissed this cockamamie fancy, embarrassed by my wistfulness, only to learn later that Mom actually had begun to warm to the idea.

It was during this sunny period that I realized my father had stopped talking about the war. The old mainstay of our relationship disappeared when he became more involved in the present, quietly retiring his regrets and ghosts. I didn't know how to see him but through the lens of World War II. How much did this father and daughter have in common after all?

For years I had kept Dad a secret, saying nothing about him to anyone outside my family. Eventually I learned that some of my friends assumed he was dead or otherwise absent from my life. I didn't hide Dad because I was ashamed of him—although I often was. Only once had I met somebody with a dad like mine, a walking wounded of World War II, and it felt like a betrayal to talk about Jerry Collins with anyone who didn't have this insight. But now, officially retired, nicely dressed, enough cash in his wallet, he was a lot more like the aging dads of my childhood pals—a regular Branford guy after all. I would have to get to know him from scratch.

One July afternoon he met me at the New Haven train station. "Welcome home, Chule," he said gaily, giving me a quick hug. It was an uncommon move—to avoid rejection he typically waited for me to approach him. He looks so cheery, I thought, beginning to relax. I always arrived home nervous, trained to expect the worst. But here was my father, all peppy and excited about something. He took my bag as we headed for curbside parking.

"Ta-da!" He waved toward an unfamiliar car. It was a white Chrysler Le Baron, a medium-sized four-door in tip-top condition and only two years old. "Your mother and I just bought it this week. I'm the sole driver, though. Her chauffeur."

"My, my, my," I said, standing back to properly admire. "What a beauty."

"Fully loaded. It's even got AC." A heat wave was on. "You won't believe how fast it pumps out the cold air."

He stowed my bag in the trunk and we climbed in, the red plush upholstery exhaling a whiff of the previous owner's cigar habit. Mom had entrusted the choice of automobile entirely to her ex-husband. I listened to his enthusiastic account of trolling the local lots and hanging tough till the dealer caved and knocked some hundreds off the price. "You wouldn't believe what I got for trading in that crummy Pacer," he boasted.

As we cruised home on silken treads, my father pointed out the fine features of our chariot. "Listen to this," he said, inserting a tape. "We've never had one of these before. A working cassette player." As Louis Armstrong crooned "A Kiss to Build a Dream On," I who now dined out regularly and wore boutique clothing felt humbled by my father's unmitigated joy in what looked like the cast-off of some blue-haired retiree making a beeline to Florida.

"This is a great car, Dad," I said. "You done good."

His blissful retirement proved short-lived. At the same time his spirits took off, his body began breaking down for good. While visiting I awoke each night to hear him coughing to the point of collapse, then stumbling downstairs to find a quiet corner where he could recover, the lung-rattling heaves finally subsiding into gentle percussion as he smoked and sucked on Smith Brothers lozenges. By day the coughing was less severe but a constant presence, shaking him into red-eyed weariness.

Then he began to lose his appetite, which had always been impressively hearty, at odds with his thin physique. Mom took over the cooking again, preparing invalid-style cuisine. He took to sitting stiffly for long periods in the chair he formerly occupied only for movie watching. Soon he was having trouble walking at all. While visiting my oldest brother's family, a number of us went en masse to the National Gallery in Washington, DC. We fell silent in mutual alarm watching Dad shuffle at a baby-steps pace across the merciless vastness of the Mall, his face twisting in pain. He spent that afternoon recovering in the museum café. "I'll—take—care—of—it," he wheezed, when I insisted he see a doctor. "My business. Get off my back, Julie, please." I reported to Mom and she shook her head mournfully. "You think I've been very hard on your father. But I always told him I'd pay the bills if he'd go in for regular checkups. And fix his teeth too, for god's sake. He's a stubborn old arse and he will not budge."

My father the Marine had chosen to clutch a grenade to his chest. He wouldn't move a finger to save himself. But he had one goal left: to attend the fiftieth reunion of his Branford High School class. For months he dragged himself to planning meetings, setting aside his self-consciousness over his missing teeth, his shuffling gait and coughing fits. I was amazed to learn he was one of the core organizers. Since when had he grown so comfortable with the prospect of putting on a name tag and swapping "here's what I did with my life" news?

"We're expecting a big, BIG turnout," he crowed one evening. We chatted about his co-organizers, the program they had planned together. Then he started to say something but stopped himself.

"What is it, Dad?"

He shot me a quick glance. "Those men I fought with who died—some of them would be going to their reunions around now. If they'd made it home I bet they'd have a lot more to boast about than I do. But I'm the father of you five kids and that's really something."

Neither of us knew what to say after that.

The reunion was a triumph, with attendance topping 80 percent of the class. With his old Branford gang Dad relived the simpler days he had loved the most, before the global conflict swept him far away. For a short while longer he rode high on the memories of that night till his war reclaimed him for the last time.

CHAPTER FOURTEEN

"THIS ROVER
CROSSED OVER"

Jerry Collins in his formal US Marine Corp uniform

I used to walk in the shade,
With those blues on parade.
But I'm not afraid
This Rover crossed over,
If I never have a cent,
I'll be rich as Rockefeller,
Gold dust at my feet,
On the sunny side of the street.

("On the Sunny Side of the Street")

By the time of Dad's fiftieth high school reunion, I noticed with alarm that he was habitually swigging from bottles of thick pink goo. "For his stomach aches," Mom explained. "They're getting worse." In fact, the pains were warning signs of a time bomb ticking in his chest.

Soon it was Thanksgiving and he was slumped at the dining table in obvious discomfort, his hands unsteady as he performed his traditional turkey-carving duty. Mom had set Angy's flowery old English platter and bone-handled carving utensils before him, to save him the walk into the kitchen. I could barely eat for studying my dad, wondering why he was willing to endure such suffering rather than risk a doctor's help. I don't even recall who else was at the table, or which of my siblings had made the melancholy trip home. I only remember Dad grimly gumming soft mouthfuls of pumpkin pie while I thought about strong-arming him into a trip to the ER. It was a useless fantasy, however, for if any of us had dared broach the topic of doctors my gentle, recessive father would have turned to hostile steel.

Ignoring his health hadn't mattered much when he was young and fit. Now it clearly meant an early grave. The war had some mysterious role in this. Up until combat my father tolerated doctoring and occasional hospital procedures like anyone else. That changed from Okinawa onward, after he watched the corpsmen, or trained medics, desperately plugging and patching bashed and torn-up boys on the spot. He never voluntarily submitted to medical care again. It was okay with him if his body decayed and fell off in pieces: he didn't consider himself worth sewing back together.

After that gloomy holiday I returned to Boston. A few nights later I got the call from Mom: my father was undergoing emergency surgery for an aortic aneurysm, and might not survive.

He did, but not for long. The ex-insurance salesman had beaten death by an aneurysm only to learn his biggest liability had gone undetected for sixty-eight years: a congenital hole in his heart.

From the moment he entered hospital care, all the precious pleasures of Dad's short retirement fell away. He never again wore his good suit or sat behind the wheel of that Chrysler Le Baron. The A-Bay Gang had to convene without the General, his counter seat empty because he'd been yanked back into combat. It was 1945 all over again.

While he lay in animal-eyed terror at Yale New Haven Hospital, confusing the ICU with a Japanese prison camp, I became infected with his vivid paranoia. At night I dreamed of elaborate rescue attempts. In one I had mysterious leg wounds, received in some skirmish, and was trying to crawl to him, substituting the concrete "Q Bridge" that carried I-95 into New Haven for the exposed muddy plain of Okinawa. In that nightmare I crawled for some interminable amount of time, spurred on by my father's anguished cries. The bridge extended forever, it seemed, through the incessant noise of passing cars and buses. I kept shouting, hoping he'd hear me above the roaring din: "It's okay, Dad! Hold on! I'm coming! I'll get there soon!" I had this same nightmare repeatedly but I never got to the end of the bridge. Dad's voice always started to fade as my heart began to burst from hopeless exertion.

After they'd reamed and patched him up as best they could, the Yale doctors shipped my father home. There he declined steadily, with Marine-style stoicism, confined to a hospital bed in the living room, a walker waiting nearby, a commode concealed by a discreet screen Mom had painted and decorated. His face was grey with suffering and even his hair looked as though it ached, shooting up in white spikes. He had always resembled Alfalfa, the skinny cowlicked crooner from *The Little Rascals*; now I pictured a decrepit Alfalfa stashed away in some old folks' home, his singing days gone forever. My invalid father, onetime whistler, hummer, and voh-doh-dee-oh-doh-er said little and smoked nonstop. Mom emptied the chunky glass ashtray every few hours, but the whole house reeked of spent butts. She grew quieter, too, from broken sleep and constant worry. She lavished care on him, setting out a loud bell for him to summon her with during the night. Often she didn't bother with her own bed, preferring to spread out a sleeping bag on the floor near her ex-husband.

Christmas was a dazed vigil. One extraordinary act stands out, however. My mother somehow managed to buy gifts, which she signed "Love from Mom and Dad," and, to the grandchildren, "Love from Babci and Grandfather." For the first time in years I was able to thank Dad for a present. Mom had finally let go of her rage and given my father back his old role in the Collins Christmas pageant.

On New Year's Eve I was back in Boston where Seth and I lived among his enormous family. After rounds of martinis we took turns telephoning friends and relatives to sing holiday greetings. I dialed Branford and we serenaded my parents with "Auld Lang Syne." Then I put the receiver to my ear and heard my father sobbing. "That was just lovely, Julie," Mom said hoarsely, talking very fast. Her voice sounded wet from weeping. "Absolutely beautiful. Please thank everyone for us. You'll have to excuse me now, darling. I was in the middle of giving your father an enema and I need to make him comfortable. He has had the most awful constipation." I hung up the phone, fighting tears, despising myself for forcing misguided holiday cheer on my dying dad. "They loved it," I told the group.

No more pretending: all that remained was to ease my father's way out of the world. I got him stronger pain medication. Mom kept him stocked in cigarettes. I bought him a TV for company during sleepless nights. I made tape recordings of Dad's warped and weary record collection, which he hadn't been able to play in years, not since the Magnavox system he'd purchased had made its way to the Branford dump. He spent hours listening to the cassettes on a Walkman my sister gave him, propped up with pillows and smoking away, his eyes closed as Satchmo or Glenn Miller or Tommy Dorsey or Clancy Hayes lulled him into semiconsciousness. The LPs were in rotten condition so the tapes crackled and hissed nonstop, but Dad didn't seem to notice.

His feet gradually turned purple-black, the stain of death seeping slowly from his big toes to their neighbors and upward. His physical therapy regimen left him sweaty and writhing, his shrunken chest heaving ineffectually. When he tried to use the walker he gasped with each step. As the pain worsened he started keeping the TV on at all times, the volume down low. He switched channels restlessly, seeking diversion, unable in his discomfort to concentrate on a single show. I sat next to him, watching snippets of *Columbo*, nature and science programs, *MASH* reruns, and news reports. No movies, though—he couldn't stick with them, even his beloved black-and-white oldies.

One evening this World War II relic and I paused on the surreal spectacle of Raytheon "smart bombs" plummeting down airshafts. The Gulf War was on. The veteran of Operation Iceberg was incredulous over Operation Desert Storm. "Where's the desert? Where's the fighting? Why don't they show the real thing? What kind of war is this?" He was sliding into the past again. "During

World War II nobody wanted to know what really happened in combat. They weren't sending home graphic photos of bodies hit by mortar fire. But at least the fact that people were dying wasn't kept a great big secret."

He had heard on the news that some National Guard reserves were in an uproar because they'd been ordered overseas. "They got a lot of nerve," Dad fumed. "They've enjoyed the privileges and now that they're asked to serve, they balk. They made a promise, god damn it!" Suffering had shortened his fuse and made him uncharacteristically hawkish. He even looked like a hawk—his nose sharpening into a beak as the rest of his face slowly collapsed. Dad was disgusted by this war for oil and he mocked President Bush's "silly saber rattling." But my father belonged to the Greatest Generation, and the idea of shirking one's patriotic duty was abhorrent to him. It didn't matter how base the cause was; those Guardsmen had to do their duty.

The last weekend of Dad's life I came home to tend to his needs and spell my mother. I emptied the commode and ashtray, answered his bell, washed him and helped him into fresh pajamas. He tried to perform his exercises while I counted repetitions, but even as I exhorted him to "keep going, keep going, Dad," I could see it was becoming impossible. He mustered the grit to stump about with his walker but that only lasted a minute, till he nearly fainted from the weight bearing down on his poor feet.

His eyes were red rimmed with exhaustion, his body trembling. I urged him to take a nap and he said he'd try. "Don't look so worried, Chule. It's just a bad case of phoozma," he joked, referring to his made-up malaise. I faked a laugh. While I pulled down shades, adjusted his pillows, and lowered the bed he tried to say something else. He stopped and looked at me, stricken.

"What is it, Dad?" I studied his face, wondering if the pain was suddenly worse.

Tears rolled from his eyes. "Thanks for coming home, kiddo. I'm not sure why you still bother. I know I've let you all down, all of you kids, and your mother. Everything she's ever said about me, the terrible things I did, how I failed you all, is the truth."

I tried to shush him like a child, stroking his forehead, making my voice gentle. "Dad, it's okay. Don't let the past upset you." I even lied. "You have nothing to apologize for."

He went on stubbornly, about the distance between him and some of us kids, how he understood but hoped we would come round and forgive him. "I was planning to write to each of you," he said. I listened, amazed and dubious, while he talked about the five of us in turn, and the state of our lives. For all his mute invisibility he'd been keeping track. He was particularly worried about two of "the boys" who he felt he'd let down the most. "They don't really want to talk to me and I don't blame them," he said. "I messed it all up, Julie. And now look at me—I'm falling apart. I thought I would have time to make amends."

Sure you did, I thought bleakly. Well, you waited too long. I tried to say soothing, reassuring things, holding his hand, working hard to keep from whimpering. Finally he calmed down and fell quiet.

While Dad slept I told my mother I wanted to make the best Sunday dinner he could eat: roast chicken with stuffing and sides of mashed potatoes, glazed carrots, and a chopped salad with the lurid orange dressing he liked. I had leaned vegetarian since childhood and disliked handling uncooked meat, so Mom offered to tackle the raw bird for me. "No, I'll do it. I want to," I said.

When the meal was ready, Dad insisted on walkering to the kitchen table. That ordeal killed his appetite for a while, so Mom and I ate at a snail's pace to let him catch up. After dinner he sat smoking while I gave him a much-needed haircut, draping a bath towel over his knobby shoulders. "No more mountain man," I said cheerily, as I nervously combed and cut. My father had always been fastidious about his looks, despite his ruined smile. He got very fussy about that final haircut, asking for the mirror, pointing out stray or uneven bits. I wondered how he felt, staring at his face in the glass and seeing it already settling into the bony impersonality of a death mask.

At nine o'clock I kissed them goodbye and drove away, rising into the dark embrace of the old trees. I thought of all the times Dad had shuttled me to and from the train station. He had always acted so confoundingly pleased to see his standoffish, judgmental elder daughter. It didn't matter how much I held back to protect myself, and how much that hurt him. He loved me anyway.

A mile and a half up the road from our house I was stopped at the Armory intersection while a slow-moving line of military vehicles passed by. The dark shining mound on a flatbed caught my attention. It was unmistakably some kind of sea creature. An inquisitive street light picked out the dead black eye of a small whale that must have taken a wrong turn somewhere, winding up in Long Island Sound, maybe even the river, poor doomed thing. I accelerated and fell in behind the flatbed, the sharp lines of the stilled tail visible now as I distinguished the cold weighty flesh from the flickering insubstantial shadows of trees and houses lining Montowese Street.

A strange, explicit fear shot through me: I saw my father, the restless scout-observer, stranded in that rented bed, his dimming eyes seeking relief in the commotion of the TV screen, his weakening limbs pinned under the blankets. I heard him wheezing and fighting for air, the burning cigarette falling from slack fingers. I quickly pulled the car over at a pay phone, watching the whale sail off into the pensive quiet of Sunday night while I waited for my mother to pick up. "Mom? Is everything okay there?"

"Julie! To what do we owe this pleasure?" She sounded quite gay. "Your father and I were watching television together, but he fell asleep. I think he's feeling more hopeful. All thanks to your visit." The relief made me instantly exhausted.

Mom's voice changed. "Julie? Everything all right?"

"Of course." I asked her to pass a message on to my father. "I'm mailing him those mysteries I mentioned. They'll come in a few days. And I'll send him some articles I wrote." I nearly told her about the whale, its fatal wrong turn. I wanted to ask her to watch for a story about it in the *Branford Review*. I didn't, though, because then she might intuit why I'd really called. "Give Dad a kiss goodnight for me," I said. "Tell him I will try to come home this Friday."

Three days later he was dead. He had checked into the hospital again, to await a second round of heart surgery and a foot amputation. No more, the combat veteran vowed. No resilience of youth would carry him through this time. He quietly surrendered. I telephoned my mother's office minutes after she ran out the door to see her Jerry one last time, to kiss his blue lips and run her big tender fingers through his hair. Four hours later I arrived in Branford and we both stood staring at the vacant bed. She had already taken away his ashtray for washing. The bell sat silent and useless. Ring-a-ling-a-ling—"Oh, Bla-anche," I heard him chirrup one last time, putting on his ritzy voice, a last gasp of his silly side. "Go fetch me my pipe and slippers. And a box of bonbons, now there's a good girl."

That night, when I was near sleep, my father shuffled to my bedside, a near-skeleton swaddled in overlarge striped pajamas. I could see the whitened stubble on his chin and cheeks shimmering in the strange phantom light of deep night. His hair was a mess and his eyes sunken, but he was on his feet. "You can walk," I mumbled. He stroked my forehead and said, "It's okay, Chule. I'm okay. I don't want you crying about me." Then he said, "I left you something important." We looked at each other for a moment. He smiled, still missing those teeth, and faded away.

"Yeah, yeah. Sure, sure," I thought, miserable. "Same old big-talkin' Dad." One last ludicrous hint at treasure, some secret legacy he'd managed to squirrel away. I began to drift off, still grousing, wounded by his final empty promise. Something prodded me back to consciousness, however. I felt compelled to get up. After making sure Mom was asleep, I went into Dad's room to move among his things, picking them up and putting them down. Dust coated everything; the room had been uninhabited for so long. I coughed and shivered, feeling the cold close in. The room rattled with unfinished thoughts and dreams gone off the rails. I recalled summer twilight in a drowsy nursery, Dad's mellow baritone lulling two young girls to sleep before the war swooped in and plucked him away. Finally I pulled out that ratty suitcase and looked inside, my first invasion of a dead man's privacy. I found faded words and photos.

Dad's obituary, published in the *Branford Review* and the *New Haven Register*, was terse and to the point—not a lot in that life story to trumpet. I had dreaded the black-and-white summation of my poor father's meager output as a postwar man, but the obit nicely glossed over his sales career to concentrate on family ties and World War II service.

The day of Dad's funeral some local Marines presented Mom with an American flag precisely folded in a presentation box. The service was a quick and muted affair. While the organ wheezed through some hymn, I sang my father's theme song to myself: "But I'm not afraid—this Rover crossed over." I sat out the Holy Communion, watching the steady stream of believers troop up to the altar. I imagined Dad sitting next to me, uninterested in the proceedings, bored by the droning priest and longing for a smoke, cup of black coffee, friendly chat with someone on the street—the modest daily pleasures of Branford.

Breaking with Catholic and Collins tradition, Mom had asked for cremation, her ex-husband's preference. He hadn't wanted his body moldering underground, trapped in a tight-fitting box. So there were no casket and pallbearers, no procession to the cemetery. Only the usual, weirdly sociable postfuneral buffet back at 101 PO, a generous spread of cold cuts and salads and rolls from Castellon's Bakery, some homemade goodies brought over by longtime neighbors who'd recently resumed socializing with Mom and Dad. A couple of mourners got sloppy drunk on the moderately priced booze and jug wine, their jovial behavior lightening up the affair. I noted the unfamiliar faces, of friends Dad had made only in the last year or so.

Several men from the A-Bay Gang came forward to tell me what a great guy the General was. "He sure liked to have a good time," one of them said. "Always joking. And the waitresses loved him—a big tipper."

They also told me how proud he was of his progeny. "Jerry talked all the time about you kids. You gave him a lot to boast about," said one fellow, squeezing my shoulder. "He kept pictures of you all, in his wallet." That surprised me: Dad had never asked me for a recent photo and I have no idea how he got one. I meant to find out which of the guys was his great pal Dino but I had already run out of words.

"Thanks so much for coming," I said.

A death always turns into an inventory. Dad's was quick: eyeglasses, a hand puppet, Dino's seagull painting, a vinyl briefcase, some gift pens, a leather day planner, a portable alarm, a stack of *National Geographic*s, an eight-by-ten glossy of my sister taken at Hampshire College, some cards from his little girls, his precious suitcase. The wardrobe crowded with old clothes and the few recent purchases, everything neatly hung.

The night of the funeral Dad's firstborn and namesake went upstairs alone to fill trash bags with the shabby suits, ties, shoes, underwear. Jeremiah took on the morbid task to spare Mom and the rest of us. After he and his family returned to Washington, after everybody was gone but Mom and me, she begged me to haul the bags back in from the street, open them all up, and double-check the clothing for any overlooked memento. Something stashed in a pocket, perhaps. There was nothing. Then she asked me to go through the boxes of useless hardware and other old stock he'd stored in his room, but nothing turned up there either. "Please give the room one last going-over," she pressed wearily. "Then we'll call it quits and haul everything away."

Rifling through Dad's file cabinet I found one overlooked item, a cheap composition book, and flipped through the pages. They were all blank except for the draft of a letter he'd been composing that fall. It was dated about a week before the aneurysm burst. He was writing the IRS, his old nemesis, to ask for forbearance and an installment payment plan. After polite preliminaries he went on like this:

> I intend to pay everything I owe the government despite my disagreement with some calculations. However, I have additional debts I must also erase. My ex-wife Blanche G. Collins has had to advance me large sums, which I want to repay as soon as possible.
>
> In the last few years my earning potential has grown negligible. My health is poor, and although I sometimes have good days it is often difficult for me to get out of bed in the morning. I was a Marine in World War II, and that experience continues to cause me some problems. I write this to explain my circumstances, not to ask for special treatment. I propose paying a monthly amount of—

After I read the letter I shrieked and hurled the notebook across the room. Fortunately Mom was out doing errands, forcing herself back into the driver's seat. By the time she returned I had burned Dad's letter with his Bic lighter in a fit of melodramatic anguish. I threw away the notebook so she wouldn't search it, in her guilty grief still hunting for meaningful parting words, and wave it at me, opened at the torn-out pages, demanding to know what I was keeping from her.

"She's going to be fine," my brother-in-law had whispered reassuringly, on the night of the funeral. He knew I was worrying about how Mom would fare without Dad, her betrayer, her beloved, the man she had fought and lived with for over four decades. It hurt her to find no traces of the years they had spent together. They had barely made peace when he disappeared from the battlefield, the young Marine and the old man merging at the end of life. When my father's life burned away all that remained of substance waited in one old suitcase, echoes of the war that always took him from us.

EPILOGUE I'LL BE
SEEING YOU

Julia Collins and her son, Aidan

I'll be seeing you
In all the old familiar places
That this heart of mine embraces
All day through...

("I'll Be Seeing You")

In late December 1992, less than two years after my father died, my brother Jeremiah asked the Branford police to check whether anything was wrong at 101 PO because Mom wasn't answering the phone. The officers found her lying dead in the empty bathtub, fully clothed. From the look of things she'd suffered a violent, alcohol-induced attack and climbed into the tub in lieu of her bed, using the bathmat as a cover.

We all had seen it coming: barely a month after Dad's death Mom became shifty again, fending off her children with false high spirits while she secretly tried to fill his place with her bottle. Then came the string of fender benders, small fires, warnings from her Yale boss, and calls to me—the "contact in an emergency" name in her wallet—from the police, the fire marshal, concerned friends and neighbors. After she landed in detox, this time with suspected brain damage, my oldest brother became her conservator and we confined her to an institution. When she recovered enough to go home Mom pleaded for privacy, swearing she would repair her life on her own. A few weeks later she was dead.

The Collins offspring were finally free of their heartbreaking parents. But where Dad had blinked out quietly, a burnt-out bulb, Mom was a roaring wildfire that couldn't be contained. There never was room to mourn Dad because her awesome cycle of self-destruction commanded all the attention.

Now that she was gone it shamed me to realize how little thought I had given to my father, as if my heart had checked out once his ashes were in the ground. Unlike my mother, whose finger-prints covered everything at 101 PO—the tag-sale knick-knacks and furnishings, the half-finished craft projects, boxes of family junk she'd hoarded, and even a neglected garden still carrying the torch for its green-thumbed goddess—Dad had simply vanished. I could find nothing of him to carry forward. No evidence that being a dad, my dad, was ever important to him. I'd barely had a father, and the lifelong struggle not to lose him completely had had no redemptive final act. Searching for meaning in his death, all I could find was relief that he was safe from another assault on his heart and the lop-ping off of his "poor tootsies," as he'd called them. When I left Branford after his funeral, it had been surprisingly easy to leave him behind too. After all, nobody in my regular life knew a thing about him. He was still my secret.

But as soon as Mom was cremated and interred near her Jerry, their bullet-riddled union ensured into perpetuity, my father strolled back into my thoughts as if he'd been patiently waiting for me all along.

My duties as executor of Mom's tiny estate dragged me back to Branford, where my first stop was the Collins family plot at St. Agnes Cemetery. I kicked away crusty snow and poked stubborn ice with a stick to uncover Dad's grave marker. The plain granite rec-tangle flush with the frozen ground was a war veteran's perk: paid for by the US government and carved with Jeremiah F. Collins's service dates and a flag. I decided Cpl. Collins had gotten a raw deal, my lifelong ambivalence about the Good War suddenly sharp-ening into a grudge. As soon as I got to the house, I found the flag the Marines had bestowed at Dad's funeral. Naturally Mom had saved it. I pulled the flag out of its special box, unfolded it, wadded it into a ball, and threw it in the trash.

While my siblings helped sort through what was left of the Collins homestead—a rundown house, a nibbled-away plot of land—some vintage photos I'd never seen before emerged. Here was the youthful Jerry Collins: a somber toddler with his cheery little sister; a boy leading his pet goat; a self-conscious teenager with the swept-back hairstyle he would keep for fifty years; a debonair groom and his ebullient bride. But where was my dad? Finally I found one snapshot of him and me. In the soft grey image, scratched and poorly focused, I'm not yet two, wearing a pale summer dress and tiny Mary Janes, and he crouches behind me with a sweet smile on his face, his hands supporting me because I have barely learned to walk. I stared hard at his vague face, willing it to become sharp and clear, and then I burst into tears, overwhelmed with memories of this tender daddy abruptly letting go to send me on alone.

I left Dad's boyhood home for the last time on a hazy summer afternoon. Emptied and stripped, 101 PO filled up with unresolved shadows. Dust lingered uneasily in the heavy yellow light foretelling the downpour that within minutes would drive me out of town and flood the local bridges. I locked the door and put the key under the mat for the new owners. The rusty shoe of a Collins horse, maybe the one Dad used to ride, still hung by the entryway to guarantee luck for the family within. I tapped the dinner bell Angy used to clang when her full-throttle soprano summoned her son in to dinner. It was silent now, its clapper long gone. Then I got into the car where Seth was waiting, and drove away, taking the photographs of my father.

Days later, in Massachusetts, I dreamed I was standing in the kitchen at 101 PO when the phone rang. It was Dad. "I'm not dead, Chule," he said. "I was just away for a while, on business. Tell your mother and everyone else that I'm coming home today." Elated, I tore off to New Haven in the Chrysler Le Baron to pick him up at the station. I awoke crying as the train pulled in, convinced he would not be on it, ashamed for not waiting.

My father continued to shadow me after that—a whispering, insubstantial presence. But I'd had enough of his exhausted hopes, sepia small-town memories, and war. I had fretted for years over Dad's lost future when it's supposed to go the other way—the parent worries about what lies ahead for his child. For years I had stifled my rage—at his affair with my best friend's mom, his disregard for what that did to me, his broken promises, his abdication of fatherhood, his willingness to let us kids fend for themselves—fearing the truth would crush him. Now this vague, unsettling, unreliable presence had returned, encouraged by my weak-willed sentimentality, my life-long yen for that unavailable, distant daddy. I was fed up with my father and myself. I longed to shake him off for good.

At the same time Dad was haunting me, however, a parade of fiftieth anniversaries approached, honoring the epic events of World War II. Not long after his death his war suddenly resurfaced, dramatic raw material for a spate of books, movies, documentaries, and TV talk shows. A lot of the fresh coverage annoyed me—it was too reverent, made too many heroes of ordinary men. Dad's experience had been a lot messier. His confidences weren't coherent, typeset paragraphs and dramatic photos but chunks and shards, pieces of flesh, gory and raw. He did not exaggerate; he did not enlarge his role or embroider his actions. He resisted the temptation to which many succumbed, to tell a good tale and instill some heroics into what was often a dull, disheartening life punctuated by swift and unpredictable savagery.

Compelled by America's new fixation on his era, I reluctantly began to reconsider my father's fate. As the anniversaries of famous World War II battles marched by I pored over news accounts of elderly veterans recalling their days in combat, wondering how many of the men in Dad's intelligence squad were still around. I purchased a copy of *Goodbye, Darkness*, the war memoir by his comrade William Manchester, which my father had cried over when it first came out. Before, I would never open the book for fear of what it might reveal about my dad, but now I scoured its pages, actively searching for him.

All at once I was eager to read Dad's wartime letters. I visited my brother Jeremiah, keeper of the suitcase, and brought it back to Massachusetts. Exploring its contents was like opening a tomb and finding the disintegrating artifacts of a remote and mysterious personage. As I followed Jerry Collins from boot camp to Quantico, to Camps Ritchie, LeJeune, and Pendleton, then Guadalcanal, Okinawa, Guam, and lastly Tsingtao, I met for the first time the sensitive small-town boy, the confident college student, the loving son and brother, the idealistic enlisted man. Most of this Jerry was gone before I was born; only as I neared the last of the letters did I recognize the man I'd known, the disillusioned combat vet.

I found many familiar names in Dad's correspondence—the buddies from his stories. It struck me that Manchester, renowned historian and biographer of Churchill, JFK, and MacArthur, ought to be easy to find. Surely he could tell me something to help make my fading father more real. But once I got his telephone number, it took me three months to make the call. I didn't know how to present myself or my dad to his former comrades in arms. How could I answer their questions about Dad's postwar life without betraying him or upsetting them? The biggest hurdle was the nagging suspicion I'd harbored since childhood. Dad's gloom and sorrow, his need to confide his war horrors while other men kept silent, had made me wonder as I got older whether he was concealing something unspeakable. Had he been a coward or let his buddies down in combat? Had he committed some terrible act? My speculations were disloyal, but I couldn't quell them.

On a stifling August day I finally telephoned Bill Manchester. He was in poor health and we didn't talk for long. It was enough, however, for me to know my suspicions were off base. Clearly surprised when I stammered out my worry, Manchester assured me there was no cowardly act, no notoriety. "Your father was a brave Marine," he said firmly.

Bill asked me to write a letter he could forward to the other surviving unit members. He then spread the word that the daughter of one of their own sought information. All of the men except one, who was ailing and died shortly thereafter, promptly came forward with vivid memories of Jerry Collins. They opened their hearts and probed old wounds on my behalf—"anything for Jerry." Their untarnished, fifty-year-old affection for my father took me aback, and made me rethink a life's worth of daughterly analysis tainted by disappointment.

I heard first from Tim Joyner, who became a government oceanographer after the war and wrote an acclaimed biography of Magellan. Soon letters also arrived from Bill "Pete" Peterson, a petrochemical engineer who had started his own company, Sy Ivice, a Chicago businessman, and Les Penny, an accountant, who was Dad's closest buddy in the outfit. "I loved him like a brother," Les wrote to me. Some of the men also sent along photos, news clippings, poetry, and prayers.

The common view of the outfit: Jerry Collins was a reserved fellow with a sly sense of humor. He was kind hearted and thoughtful, but sharp witted and observant too. While he took wry note of the battling egos and petty behavior of some officers and enlisted men, Jerry preferred to get along well with everyone. His old comrades spoke of his generous spirit—how he helped raise funds for the families of their unit's KIAs (killed in action) by selling the jeep John and Sy swiped, and how he accompanied a close buddy on the melancholy journey to a tiny island off the coast of Okinawa where the buddy's older brother died in combat. Jerry was considered one of the most diligent, hardworking, and trustworthy of his outfit. No matter how wretched the task, he did his part without complaint. That was a revelation: in the Collins family, Dad was the shirking grasshopper to Mom's aggrieved ant. Back in the war, however, the failed salesman had faithfully met his quota and more.

Dad's buddies welcomed me into an unusual family circle that started with their tiny intelligence unit and radiated into the larger Twenty-ninth Regiment. Even Marines who hadn't known Jerry Collins came forward. Members of the same celebrated Twenty-ninth, they were eager to shed light on Dad's part of the war, and their shared trauma on Sugar Loaf Hill. Glenn Moore, the big-hearted editor of the *Marine Family Newsletter* published a request for information from anyone who had known Jerry Collins, shared his own stories of Okinawa, sponsored me as a member of the Sixth Marine Division Association, and put me in touch with Fred Abbott, a former mortarman who lives in the next town. Fred and his wife Mary came to visit, bringing scrapbooks from Marine reunions and Fred's wartime reminiscences, which shifted from humorous to somber as the afternoon passed.

After the war, few of Dad's fellow "intelligence men" had stayed in touch. For the most part, they dispersed to resume inter-rupted lives and became absorbed in the present. They reconnected as a group more than half a century later—first in 1995 and then in 1998, when they gathered to raise Bill's spirits after his wife died suddenly and he suffered a stroke. By then Jerry Collins was already dead or he would have joined the loyal march to Bill's home in Middletown, Connecticut, less than an hour from Branford. Since that reunion these stalwarts have continued to meet when they can and keep up via telephone and e-mail.

It has been two years now since I first called Bill. I've contin-ued writing to the vets I met through him. Tim Joyner has become a particular friend and we maintain a steady e-mail correspondence. He last saw Dad shortly after the war, when he went to Branford for a weekend visit. Tim recalled how they'd goofed about in the local supermarket, bowling grapefruit down the aisles. At that point each was adrift and seeking direction. Tim would soon find his footing, however, thanks to a stabilizing marriage. A witty man of deep feelings, he went on to become a noted scholar and world traveler in contrast to my father, who abandoned his academic ambitions and stayed close to home. Yet often I perceive in Tim echoes of Dad's sharp humor, "no bull" attitude, and populism. A year ago I went with my husband Seth to the Olympic peninsula in Washington, to visit Tim and his Japanese-American wife Sumiko, known to family and friends as Mabel. Tim greeted me with a red rose from his garden. He instantly saw my father in me, he said, and as the day progressed I felt I was in the company of Dad as well as Tim.

I've also been to Middletown, to visit Bill and hear about the high-flying adventures of a former war correspondent and acclaimed writer-historian, friend to JFK and RFK, and many other famous men and women. And to collect the stories and recollections of another youthful Marine who survived the Pacific bloodbath in Dad's company.

I wish my father could see his old comrades again. I go in his stead, for his sake but also for mine. I have more visits to make, and soon. The "Greatest Generation" is passing on. I am lucky I made that telephone call before I lost the chance to meet the remaining survivors of Dad's wartime family, that irrepressible bunch of nineteen brainy misfits Bill Manchester dubbed the "Raggedy-Ass Marines."

The lives of his comrades had not derailed as my father's did. Yet they intuited why Jerry Collins was undone by his experiences on Okinawa. They said he must have experienced "survivor's guilt," as they did. In Bill's case, writing a book helped exorcise his demons. For Tim Joyner, a transcendent 1989 visit to Okinawa while researching *Magellan* enabled him to replace horrifying images with scenes of an island reborn, a peaceful society of gentle people no longer crushed between two ruthless enemies.

When World War II ended, Americans shed the communal ideals that had inspired my dad and his peers to enlist. The young fighters came home expecting to resume normal lives. But the country had changed dramatically, and so had they. For many a veteran, as for my father, war was the pinnacle, the crowning moment of valor and achievement in their lives. Peacetime was a letdown.

Readjusting was especially tough for Pacific veterans like Dad because the home front had always cared much more about the war in Europe. Pacific fighters and Marines in particular got the dregs of supplies and support. Dad's invasion, one of World War II's biggest, bloodiest battles, was also overshadowed by a barrage of events: FDR's death and Truman's first weeks in office, the fall of Berlin and Germany's surrender, the revelations of Nazi concentration camps, and the bombing of Hiroshima and Nagasaki. Emperor Hirohito's hasty surrender was the final shove that sent Jerry Collins's campaign to oblivion. His proud parents had clipped every news item on Okinawa, but once he came home they too were eager to put his ordeal to rest. He'd barely unpacked before the biggest event of his life was reduced to careful chitchat, his dead buddies glossed over.

For a Depression-era boy who had never left New England, World War II represented a stunning expansion of my father's world. He crossed America and the equator, traversed thousands of miles of ocean, island hopped in the tropics, and finally made it all the way to China, that country he told his oldest daughter she could visit too, if she dug deep enough in the yard with her miniature shovel. But when the salty vet came home in April 1946, those boundaries immediately contracted, along with his ambitions.

"The war ruined my son," my grandmother confided to my mother after she filed for divorce. "When Jerry came back he wasn't the same. He stopped caring about a lot of things. He couldn't get that war out of his system." By then Angy's relationship to her son had turned stone cold. Self-centered and ashamed of her child, she refused to reach out, lacking the loving spirit of Pop who would never have shunned his troubled son. Not until after Dad died did Mom report to me what Angy had said and admit she probably was right.

It would take a later war, in Southeast Asia, to make the public conscious of combat's psychic wounds. World War II vets did their duty long before the soul-searching of the antiwar movement or diagnoses of post-traumatic stress syndrome. Theirs was the honorable war, its brutal aspects better left unexamined. "Advance— Advance—Advance"—the Marine shout also applied to peacetime: no backward looks, no lollygagging in anguished confusion. The troubled World War II vet suffered alone with his grisly memories and sense of having left his better self behind. While Dad's ruination set him apart in his achieving generation, he shared his peers' famous reticence to put the war in personal terms—until defeat and depression drove him to reveal himself to his little girls.

The hidden war wounds that undermined his life infected our family. But in his postwar struggles, as in the real war, Dad was not alone. And neither were we. Since his death, I have come to understand that he was in the company of many men whose lives were devastated by the Good War, with repercussions that would be felt for generations. Many of the deaths set in motion by that war played out for decades, slow and excruciating. Many a family, like mine, can trace to World War II the root causes for the remoteness, anger, depression, despair, alcoholism, violence, even the suicide of their husband or father. Like my dad, the unlikeliest of warriors, many men did not belong in combat and were altered forever by its brutal exigencies.

"I left you something important," my phantom father told me on the night of his death. I'm still a nonbeliever, as was Dad, but whether his freed spirit or my own yearning came to comfort me doesn't matter. Eventually I realized Dad did leave a legacy: his suitcase full of memories, which led me to his long-lost brothers and to the Jerry Collins I had never known.

He also left behind five adult children. Caught between warring parents, we established our own esprit de corps, forged under fire not on a battlefield but in a family, in an ordinary house, in a typical town. We grew up loving our father, but rejected his lousy example and aspired to be different. Nonetheless, attributes of Dad are spread thickly among us: his sense of humor, sometimes playful, sometimes biting; his gift for music; his watchfulness; his gentleness and excessive sensitivity; his swift shifting between bravura and humility; his rooting for the underdogs of the world.

Dad's inexplicable struggles ultimately made his children more compassionate. He linked us to a war that swallowed up millions of lives and transformed its survivors forever. In Jerry Collins's case, the result was a father who was a lot less than he should have been. But even when I thought I despised him, I could no more abandon Dad than he could have left a wounded buddy on the battlefield.

At times, in anger, I scorned his sacrific—though he gave three years to the Marines, my father fought in only one invasion, after all. How could one measly battle so damage a man? Gradually I wised up to the realities: the invasion of Okinawa was a war of attrition that lasted nearly three months—a desperate, all-out expenditure of men and firepower guaranteed to shatter any young warrior's fancies of heroism and righteousness. One day of such combat sent many to the rear for psychiatric care. I'd also assumed that most World War II vets saw action, when in fact nineteen men at a distance supported each fighter at the front. Like the civilians at home, those nineteen had little notion of what they'd missed. Even the intrepid war correspondents weren't close enough to tell it like it really was. His walk through fire and blood is what bound Dad to his comrades for life, and forever isolated him from the rest of us.

Only by following Dad into his past have I finally learned what his Leatherneck pals knew all along: Jerry Collins was a decent, loyal, and courageous man. Until the clock stopped for him in 1946 he did all that was asked of him, and much more. After the war, he did what he could. It was never enough; that will never be okay. I have stopped regretting what might have been, however, and found another way into the heart of my enigmatic father, that blurred figure smiling at me from an old snapshot.

Once a year I return to our mutual hometown, looking for Jerry Collins. I drive by 101 PO, tsk-tsking again that the owners after us chopped down the shapely butternut tree where Dad used to hang the Christmas lights. I speed away and make a quick detour on the peaceful street where he was born. Then I cruise down Main Street where he marched as a newly returned vet, past the James Blackstone Memorial Library we both patronized weekly, the darkened Branford Cinema he used to patrol with his flashlight, and on to bittersweet Branford Point, the lovely setting for Collins outings, picnics, and trysts. There I make a slow circuit before zipping to the spot where Friendly's used to be, then off to the Collins cemetery plot where I scatter shells I've picked up on the beach. Sometimes I make two more stops—the childhood home of Stacey Ketchum on Collins Drive, a two-second glance all I can stomach, and the seaside lot where the Waverly Hotel, my exiled dad's temporary home, sank in squalor until a merciful fire swept it away.

All along my route I imagine the tenderhearted boy who went off to become a Marine, and the soul-weary man who came back. I think I know them both now. Dad has stepped out of the shadows and I see him clearly, the young man and the old together. Since I began writing this book, I no longer dream of screaming shells and mutilated bodies. When my first child, a son, arrives—any moment now—I will leap with him into a future I had scarcely let myself claim before, for fear of emulating Dad. For me, peace is finally possible. I have forgiven my father and found where his promise still resides. Our war is done.